ESD Dialogues

Practical approaches to Education for Sustainable Development
by and for educators

ISBN 978-91-7569-929-5

9 789175 699295

Authors: Marilyn Mehlmann and Olena Pometun
Design: Vahram Muradyan
Publisher and printer: BoD

Marilyn Mehlmann · Olena Pometun

ESD
Dialogues

Practical approaches to Education for Sustainable Development
by and for educators

SWEDEN

GLOBAL
ACTION
PLAN®

CONTENTS

FOREWORD

Effective teaching – and therefore effective learning – for sustainable development: what have we learnt about it? This innocuous question has unfolded into several others:

- What is needed to create effective curricula or programs for different audiences?

- What does it take to deliver the programs successfully?

- How do we need to think about enabling the programs to disseminate rapidly?

- How can we understand the transformative essence – and power – of sustainable development?

- And, not least, how can we plant within the programs the seeds of their own transformation?

This book explores the questions to the best of our present understanding. Hopefully it too contains the seeds of its own transformation.

YOU, THE READER

This book is mainly for educators and researchers interested in the particular pedagogical requirements of teaching and learning for sustainable development, whether in or outside the formal education sector. Please view it as a 'work in progress', an exploration of the above questions.

US, THE AUTHORS

We, the authors, are two people who have approached ESD from different perspectives: Olena Pometun as a member of the educational establishment in a post-Soviet world, Marilyn Mehlmann as an informal teacher and trainer of adults in Western Europe. We found common ground in the seminal question: How is it possible to educate 'everyone' FOR sustainable development? What pedagogical methods, approaches, tools, skills are required to bring about the transformation implied in the phrase 'education for sustainable development'?

1. STARTING POINTS

For the purposes of disseminating a functioning educational program, clearly the established educational institutions have a strong advantage over informal education structures. However these institutions also pose the greatest challenge when it comes to introducing significantly new approaches. So we start with Olena's reflections.

Experiences that changed our views of the role of education

Olena:

In my work as professor at the National Academy of Pedagogical Science in Kiev – a research academy – I have worked for years to find effective forms and methods of interactive pedagogy, and teach them to teachers. We have made, I believe, some progress in influencing the post-Soviet school system. Then, in 2005, my colleagues and I began working on the practical implementation of ESD in Ukrainian schools. We quickly came to the conclusion that our cherished (and successful) interactive pedagogies were not sufficient for this task.

So what were the problems? Well, they had something to do with the pedagogy; and the solutions we found, together with colleagues from Global Action Plan, are what this book is mainly about.

They also had (and have) a lot to do with the education system. Firstly, there was an automatic assumption that ESD belongs in the realm of natural science. Secondly, the trans-disciplinary nature of ESD is foreign to the structure of most school curricula.

TRANSDISCIPLINARITY OF ESD BRINGS PROBLEMS

In a conventional educational context in post-Soviet countries, transdisciplinarity means introducing elements from many different school subjects. But where does ESD belong?

Ukrainian educators traditionally connect SD to the sphere of natural science. And there is certainly something in this. For example ESD students can definitely benefit from their classes in chemistry (composition of water, air), physics (measuring of energy and power), biology, and other knowledge about nature.

However, ESD also demands great attention to social aspects, because a sustainable society cannot function without democracy, on-going dialogue, participation, and the empowerment of people – individuals and groups. Also SD is only possible when human relationships are based on respect, tolerance, intercultural cooperation. So from the perspective of the standard school curriculum this is already 'social studies' and even social psychology, social 'engineering', or even philosophy. And in the case of ESD, not only elements of such subjects are integrated but also a lot of information from and about everyday life. So we needed to create a special new integrative and inclusive subject, and implement it within a completely different model of school education.

Such a situation raises questions at every point in the development and dissemination of ESD programs. Which teachers shall teach it? As part of what subject? What other subjects might it take time from? Who decides?

All of these problems can be solved, or at least mitigated, by viewing ESD as an extra-curricular subject in an educational situation where both teachers and pupils volunteer. And indeed, in many situations this can be the best or only solution. But... surely ESD is meant to be for everyone? This was our starting point: to create a program that could be accepted and integrated as a regular part of the school curriculum.

This leads to a practical and important challenge for schools: which teachers will deliver the ESD course? In our experience the first candidates who present themselves are mostly teachers of biology and geography, with experience of environmental education. Consequently, they are happy to emphasize environmental topics rather than embracing the whole of SD. So sometimes the purpose of the ESD course is understood better by teachers of history, school psychologists, and social pedagogues because they are not locked into an "environmental stereotype". The challenge is to find, motivate and train them – and to help create opportunities for them in their schools.

Marilyn:
Meantime I was coming from a different direction, having worked since the mid 1980s with questions related to sustainable lifestyles. At that time we called it 'ecological living' – the expression 'sustainable development' didn't really take root until after the United Nations conference in Rio de Janeiro in 1992.

PRODUCING BEHAVIOUR CHANGE

In 1989 we produced the first version of a behaviour-change program for adults and households, called the Household EcoTeam Program. New elements were added year by year, the most distinctive being a program to train and introduce coaches to each team of households. Gradually it became apparent that the program was producing extraordinary results; and also that the results could not be conveyed through the words alone. Groups in several countries translated the materials; but without any true understanding of the underlying principles it seemed they had only a 50/50 chance of success.

So then began a long process of identifying the most important design principles, and designing a program for cultural adaptation.

SUCCESSFUL ADAPTATION

By 1998 we felt confident we could introduce the household program into a new culture with 100 % success – and we had reduced adaptation time from (typically) four years, to 11 months.

We had also analysed and synthesized success factors from a dozen or more different programs in different countries, and begun teaching them not only to our colleagues but also to other NGOs; been the object of considerable research, notably in the Netherlands and the UK; and begun experimenting with programs for children and youth. In particular, our colleagues in Poland developed very successful programs for children and schools.

So by the time we met our Ukrainian colleagues in 2003, we had a lot of material, methods and experience to offer. And we quickly understood that they also had a lot to contribute.

Olena:

The idea of sustainable development is not yet well known in Ukraine. My own awareness of its depth and significance also took time. Today, very important for me is the universality, the globality of this development path for humankind and every single human being, its true, deepest humanism: the possibility it offers to combine the interests of any individual, group, and society in general with each other in a very surprising and harmonious way at different levels. As I see it, society, on a path of sustainable development, can create an optimally comfortable environment for everyone - in the social, economic, environmental and spiritual dimensions.

Seen in this light, ESD allows us to glimpse a way to construct a new content for education, focused on the future of humankind and every individual's potential to participate in creating that future. In doing so, we need to prepare students to be carriers of cultural creativity, not merely good performers. The truth is that the school has no future if it cannot cope with this task. And this is not a question of major scientific discoveries, which only few can achieve. It is the ability to create a truly sustainable society for themselves and others, rather than competing with each other for power or resources.

We are talking about a gradual transformation of the entire education system: new goals, new content, new methods, forms of training, new ways of interaction between students and teachers.

The principles for empowering programs proposed by GAP enabled us to approach the development of the course "Lessons for sustainable development" from a fundamentally different teaching position. Our attempts to create content and methodology for schools on that basis has enabled us to take a fresh look at many of the traditional theories and practices of teaching.

The best is not good enough - yet

Olena:
What were those new, different ideas, which we have found in ESD, and which are not even included in the best practices of existing schools?

First of all, there is a link to the social climate: relationships and interaction between participants in the learning process. These characteristics are largely inherent to interactive learning as we have come to understand it. Key characteristics are:
- *Respect for the personality of the child, his/her thoughts, feelings, which is reflected in listening, invitation to reflection, constant feedback, and support.*
- *Permanent involvement of all pupils into the process, underlining the value of everyone's participation.*
- *Stimulating pupils' activity by asking questions, rather than giving answers.*
- *Productive and tolerant cooperation and communication between pupils as the basis for class work.*
- *Trust in the pupils, which enables the teacher to offer them choices, in or outside the classroom, concerning actions, time, resources, etc.*
- *Absence of pressure to achieve, obligatory participation in all activities, stressful competition, and negative feedback.*

Our experience shows that this model can be implemented quite successfully, provided that the teacher is well prepared and the curriculum is not overloaded. It is, in fact, not so difficult for teachers to refrain from assigning fragmented tasks and giving long explanations on how to do them, but instead to offer students an integral problem; and to create the conditions for resolving it, such as tutoring, and offering necessary information as well as an opportunity for a discussion.

However, we must say that interactive education in Ukrainian schools is often presented as the best practices of individual teachers or as a model for teaching particular subjects, not as a generally effective model. In reality, active learning tends to entail significant organizational efforts from the teacher. Tight regulation of communication during the lesson remains the norm, with a concentration of efforts by both teachers and pupils on acquiring knowledge and skills to meet external state requirements.

And even beyond interactive education, ESD requires some pedagogical characteristics that are not present in the Ukrainian school system:
- *Orienting the learning process towards the real-life needs of students today; absence of unnecessary information, the kind that is learnt "just in case".*

- *Connecting individual and collective goals of students with the goals of their community, country and all humankind.*
- *Goals both for life and for learning are set by students themselves during and as a result of learning.*
- *Organic relationships between real life and learning, literally flowing into one another.*
- *Open style of learning, when any information brought by the pupil is treated as meaningful, including his/her own thoughts, the thoughts of other people, especially family members, their experience and actions. Openness gives space for innovations and surprises. We are not only confident that the future will be better, but we also understand that we cannot predict how it will come about.*
- *Assessment of individual results of the student without comparing them to the results of others.*

Finally, ESD is fundamentally different from all current educational theories and practices in the Ukraine, because it suggests that students will overtake their teachers. And if at some point the teacher becomes sure that s/he knows much more than the students, and that s/he can teach everything - s/he is no longer an ESD teacher.

In these and other psychological and pedagogical characteristics, ESD differs from educational theories and models I have come across so far. It empowers our students and helps them consolidate new behaviours and patterns of thinking.

Things happen when they are meant to. Now we have a choice. We can continue using traditional educational approaches; or, if we are ready, we can create a new sustainable future in every lesson.

Marilyn:

As in Ukraine, so in many countries. And as in schools, so in society at large.

As regards ESD in Swedish schools, for instance, we often hear that 'we're already doing it'; when what is actually being done may be closer to environmental education, and the pedagogy, while impressive, nonetheless falls short of the transformational aspects underlined by Olena.

Concerning adult education there is a slightly schizophrenic attitude on the part of many people responsible for or involved in ESD. On the one hand, we often hear 'You can't teach old dogs new tricks,' 'You can't change people's behaviour.' This is clearly nonsense, since all of us change our behaviour all the time - just think for a moment about your own daily habits 5 or 10 years ago (what, no cell-phone??). While on the other hand, there seems to be great and unwarranted faith in the power of information to generate behaviour change.

In GAP we started asking ourselves why and how we DO change our behaviour. Over twenty years, that enquiry has led to the principles for empowering programs on which the Ukrainian and all new GAP programs are based.

This is not to say that we are satisfied. We are happy with our results to date - and we want to do better in the future. So the search for the truly pivotal elements continues.

2. A JOURNEY OF EXPLORATION

The search for a pedagogy for SD is thus an on-going journey of exploration, in which more and more people are joining. Like 'sustainable development' itself, it presents a huge challenge, and many adventures.

Questions about long-term behaviour change

Marilyn:

The whole concept of sustainable development depends for its success on wide-spread behaviour change: the public (general, or employees, customers, suppliers, managers, politicians…) need to change their behaviour in step with the introduction of technical and socio-economic changes.

Attempts to bring about wide-spread behaviour change sometimes succeed but often don't. Moreover, outcomes are difficult to predict. For example, the economists' homo oeconomicus model, based on the idea that every person at all times tries to maximize financial benefit to him-/herself, gives at best only weak predictability. For most people this is understandable. I personally have never met anyone who lives in accordance with this model - there are so many other factors in our lives than money. Nonetheless it is widely used in economics and forms the basis for many business and political decisions; including behaviour-change campaigns.

There is a mental map of the behaviour change terrain that is widely accepted – or rather, taken for granted. It is linear and generally mechanistic, with roots in models from natural science (and indeed from classical military engineering). It constitutes the unspoken basis for many small and large information campaigns with the intention of bringing about long-term behaviour change - regardless of whether their focus is on PR, marketing, or social information.

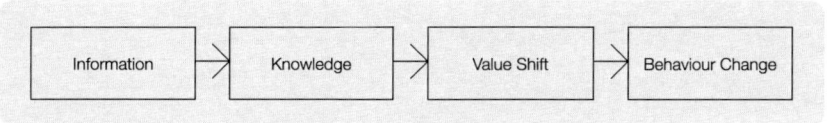

Figure 1. A linear model of behaviour change

This model has a number of deficiencies that create or contribute to problems, e g

- *It is energy-intensive and expensive; it can be compared to growing plants in a greenhouse, with a constant need to bring in supplies of nutrients, water and energy*
- *It presupposes that a person or a small group - those telling people what to do - knows and can unambiguously describe exactly which behaviour changes will produce the desired results*
- *It builds on the assumption that target groups will adopt the desired behaviours more or less unconsciously*

- *It often builds on an unspoken assumption that what is good for the group ("society") is automatically also good for the individual*
- *It interacts with a mental picture of "motivation" as a transitive verb – something one person does to another – and thus misses the opportunity to engage self-motivating creativity*

This linear approach to behaviour change is costly and typically run as 'one off' campaigns over a limited time period. When the campaign is over, it's over.

Typical residual result (retained behaviour changes in the target group after the campaign is finished) is around 12–15 %. Maybe most importantly, this model has only one intervention point: providing information – in an already information-stressed environment.

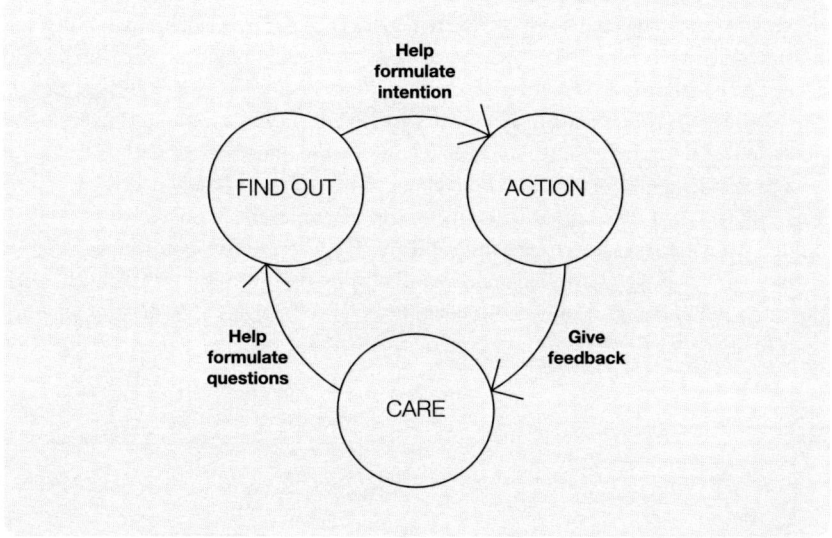

Figure 2. A circular or spiral model of behaviour change

If the linear model were the only or best model for producing widespread behaviour change, the outlook would be bleak. However, action research undertaken by GAP over two decades, and backed by academic research in several countries, demonstrates that there are alternatives. The current basis for our program design is a spiral model (Figure 2).

This model suggests that when you care about something, you are likely to look up information about both the problem(s) and possible effective actions - things you can do in order to make a difference. Having done so you may be able to care more, and round you go. In the best case you are not only going round, but also 'up' a spiral of increasing scope to care and thus to take action.

Results from over 15 years' experience of programs working in this way (EcoTeams and other programs) suggest that this model has a residual result of more than 90% after finishing the program – and then rising to over 100% due to new, sustainable habits acquired by the same people.

So not only is the approach six times more effective – it also offers six intervention points instead of only one, as illustrated in the diagram and described in more detail in 'Characteristics of Empowering Programs'.

Can methods make such a difference?

If sociological surveys of behaviour-change programs give rise to pessimism when considering the challenges of sustainable development, how is it that GAP-inspired programs seem to produce such different results? WWF, for instance, in an excellent report Weathercocks and Signposts, could be interpreted as postulating that individually motivated behaviour change simply doesn't work - and indeed can lead us further into UNsustainable development.

Very often, pessimists and critics have been evaluating behaviour-change programs designed according to the linear model. As outlined above, such programs require high inputs of information and money; when the inputs disappear, so does most of the newly-acquired behaviour. There are of course exceptions, for instance the Swedish campaign promoting use of car seat belts; but they tend to be exceptionally long, and accompanied by punishment for people failing to comply.

Our work is based on an empowering approach (described in the next section, pp xx) involving peer support – closer to what is sometimes referred to as 'community-based social marketing' (CBSM). Such an approach may also require high inputs, of time and money; for example in the form of recruiting teams and coaching them. However the difference in final result is striking: a six-fold improvement in retention.

Another difference is that many linear behaviour-change campaigns target one specific behaviour, deemed to be 'sustainable'. Since a basic principle of empowerment is to offer choice, we find it necessary to work with a whole spectrum of behaviours. This also helps raise awareness about the interconnectedness of all things, and thus empowers participants to make - and continue to make - informed choices.

The major factor producing the difference seems to be the empowerment itself: new behaviour is much more likely to be retained when people are supported to make their own informed, conscious decisions, in a supportive environment. With a conventional behaviour-change approach, target groups are generally intended to change behaviour without too much reflection – and without asking too many questions. Blown by the winds of influence, they are more easily influenced by the next wind.

A spin-off effect we have often observed is that empowered people may be willing and even eager to empower others. For instance, in a trial of a particular section of the Ukrainian 'Lessons for Sustainable Development', for 14–15 year olds, we aimed to gather detailed results from 90–125 pupils. We were puzzled to receive over 600 result sheets – and then found that the original pupils were themselves 'recruiting' younger pupils and empowering them to use the materials too.

So we don't share the pessimism that says 'You can't teach old (or even young) dogs new tricks'. And yes, we believe methods can and do make a big difference.

Understanding empowerment

Marilyn:

At the heart of empowerment, in an educational context, is the relation between information and action.

A traditional view is that information, in the best case, will finally result in knowledge, which will lead to changed values or attitudes; and that this in turn will bring about changes in the behaviour of the student. But the relation between information, knowledge and action is not simple. We constantly screen out information offered to us by teachers, media, other people, and even our own experience. If it doesn't "fit" with what we believe we already know, we reject it.

Why be surprised when some new scandal breaks showing that scientists have manipulated the "facts" to suit what they wanted to find? You and I do it all the time. Admittedly a scientific education is supposed to teach how not to do that, but it generally misses out one very important factor: not only our minds but also our beliefs and feelings are involved in the conversion of facts to knowledge.

What I know is good, and what I don't know is no problem because I can find out. The problems come with what I believe, or think I know.

Much education and most information campaigns are designed along the traditional, mind-focused model (Figure 1, above). It all seems very logical. But we also know that it's a poor model of reality. We inform and inform, for example about the risks of smoking. If the traditional model were an accurate picture of reality, there would hardly be a smoker left in the world today.

In practice almost the opposite seems to be true. Each of us is bombarded with gigantic amounts of information every day, maybe hundreds of thousands of times as much as we can actually absorb. Somehow, each of us decides what to hear and what to activate.

A CIRCULAR RELATION

One way to understand what goes on is to view information and action as two elements in a circular or even spiral relationship. The third element is attention, or caring. It works like this:

- *I take in information about things I care about. If you decide to buy a Fiat, you see nothing but Fiats where you saw none before.*
- *I care about things I believe I can affect by my own actions.*

Conversely, things I believe I can't influence are things I care little about; therefore I absorb little information about them – as illustrated in Figure 2 (above).

There are of course exceptions. I might be passionately interested in cars even though I see no possibility of owning one. Some people actually take in information about things they believe they can't influence, often in a limited subject area, without actually absorbing it, but rather spewing it out again over anyone who will listen. You may know someone who seems to delight in telling you that the world is about to come to an end, or the moral fibre of the country is in total collapse? Still, our experience indicates that most of us in most contexts behave in accordance with the circular diagram.

BREAKING INTO THE CIRCLE

If you want to bring about change, for yourself, or for example for your students, your school, the parents of your students, you need to break into the circle. The circular relationship can be very rigid and quite difficult to break into. Or... more correctly, it's extremely difficult to break into it only via information, as the description shows. This is where most of us try to do it, most of the time.

The good news is, the circle model offers us more options. The other two points on the circle can be more fruitful.

I can break into the circle at the point of action, which seems quite the reverse of all conventional wisdom on influencing people's behaviour. First comes the changed behaviour, then the thirst for information, then the change in attitudes and beliefs.

I can also break into the circle at the point of caring, especially if I have personal interaction with people. This is why – as the best salespeople know – the most important skill in selling is to be able to listen. And the most important skill in teaching is the ability to ask empowering questions - and to listen to the answers.

We return to this circle, or spiral, in the chapter Curriculum / program design, in the section about empowerment.

Olena:

Typically, ESD programs for children include topics related to the creation of teams, visions of the future, use of resources (garbage, water, energy, travel), consumption problems: things we buy and things we eat. These programs prove to be very successful, if they are adapted to the national system of education. For example, in Poland they exist as extra-curricular programs. Every year, several hundred teachers attend training sessions, and thousands of pupils take part in this popular program - see also the section 'Some case studies'.

However, in the Ukrainian education system, which is traditionally post-Soviet, there are some obstacles to the rapid and effective dissemination of ESD.

A major obstacle is the knowledge paradigm, which is the basis of the school system. Knowledge is considered as the only valid result of education. Our school system is mainly directed to forming the knowledge of pupils, and it succeeds very well. However, the system does not work explicitly with understanding, attitudes, behaviour, despite a growing insight that knowledge is just one part of the chain in moving from information to action.

AN EXPERIMENTAL CURRICULUM IN UKRAINE

The world's first ESD course for a comprehensive school, known as Lessons for sustainable development, has been introduced in the Ukraine as the result of successful implementation of empowering curriculum design, as introduced by Global Action Plan.

Unlike existing school courses dealing with environmental problems in theoretical and informational dimensions (Geography, Geography of Ukraine, Biology, Basics of Ecology...), the integrated trans-disciplinary educational course Lessons for Sustainable Development allows pupils to connect every topic with the concept of SD and with their ideas about the future, and to choose their own lifestyle. Experience shows that the experience of changing daily behaviour and habits not only leads to a deep understanding of SD, and one's place in moving towards it, but also to strong motivation to act in this direction.

The main components of this educational process are:
- *Independent cognition and action*
- *Self- and mutual education of the students*
- *Making independent decisions concerning one's daily life.*

The Russian and Ukrainian languages have no word that is precisely equivalent to "empowerment" in meaning. The words we use signify an awakening of one's inner power, inspiration, and motivation for action. So in literal translation we call the empowering pedagogy a "pedagogy of inspiration and action".

The main principles of this pedagogy consist in creating conditions for increasing confidence and responsibility for one's actions by the students, for the emerging of enthusiasm and satisfaction from group and individual work, of psychological comfort during the educational process, and for gaining skills to cooperate and reflect. The main task of the teacher is facilitating students' progress, i.e. encouraging and aiming/guiding their efforts.

A FEW THEORETICAL REMARKS

If we return to the linear diagram in Figure 1 above (Information input - knowledge formation - attitude change (change of value system) we see that it corresponds to a traditional approach to the kind of education that is aimed at behaviour change.

However, our observations show that such a process leads to neither values formation, nor to real behaviour change in practice. Empowering pedagogy offers ways to overcome the disadvantages of this approach. Any human action starts from the emergence of a need and a motive (a person starts caring, being concerned about something), which induces him/her to search for information for resolving the issue.

Once in possession of the information, the person makes a choice and acts. The results of the action, illuminated by genuine caring and reflection, create motivation for a new stage – which may build upon a wish to improve the efficiency of the action, to receive results faster, to set a new goal, etc. Thus the spiral continues: this is a picture of how empowerment can work. From a pedagogical perspective, we can recreate it in education by creating relevant educational situations for it to be "triggered" in every new topic (Figure 3).

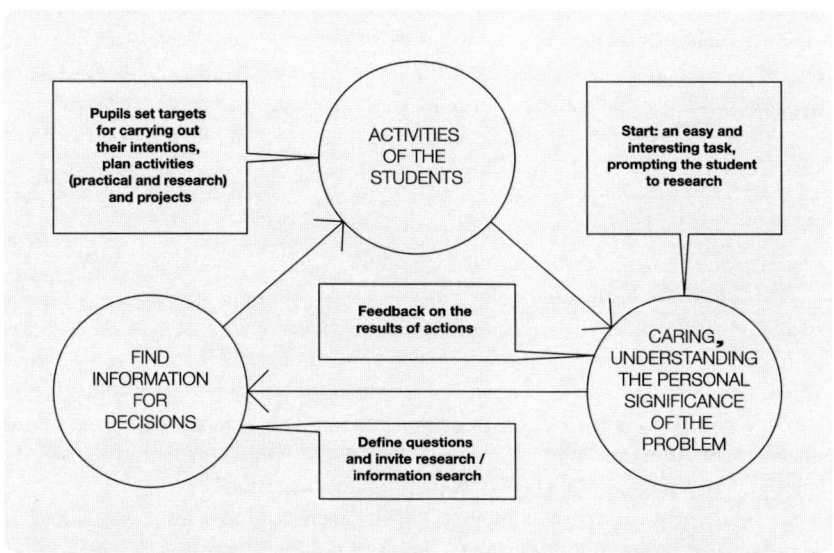

Figure 3. A model of the learning process with an empowering pedagogy.
In circles: students teaching; in rectangles: teachers teaching

STEPS IN THE PEDAGOGICAL PROCESS

Considering these psychological realities, an empowering pedagogy invites students to experiment, i.e. to take immediate action. Such an activity starts from small lifestyle research, auditing daily habits. The audit is an independent research assignment, which a student undertakes in order to chart his/her lifestyle; it is also an analysis of past experience with the help of questions suggested in the textbook. An audit is also a way to initiate a discussion in a student group, a way of entering into the topic. The student can properly understand (and, subsequently, change) something once s/he has taken some action. The main question addressed by students during such self-research is: what is my own lifestyle?

Thus, a pedagogical point of entry into the circle is an invitation to students to take experimental action (Figure 3).

These easy initial research steps reveal to students certain aspects of their contextual reality that give rise to concern, anxiety, a wish to make things better. In other words, their capacity to care is focused. Students come to a lesson with these results. In order to take the next step, the teacher offers them a small reflection exercise and invites a topic discussion.

Taking part in a discussion, students experience a need for information and formulate their own questions, for themselves and for the teachers. Formulating questions induces students to look for answers, i.e. independent knowledge search. By acquiring knowledge independently, students become better prepared for new challenges and future actions (Figure 3).

This search for information encourages the formation of an intention to start effective actions and to set concrete goals in order to get visible results. The teacher may use different ways for organizing space for such actions, e.g. inviting individual changes of daily habits, group and collective projects, researches, teaching and supporting others, etc.

Gaining results from accomplishment of the action and reflection uncovers for the student new aspects of the issue with which s/he is concerned. The wish to continue acting – "caring" – emerges when a person sees the result or believes in it. When a child understands that s/he can take effective action, s/he wants to "learn" and "care". Therefore, even when the course is over, the student, being motivated, usually decides to continue acting in this direction.

Thus, the education is focused on the perceptions, decisions and actions of students, and not on the issues as such. The aspirations and energy of the participants emerge from the inner vision of the environment and society that the participants want to live in, and not from the fear of environmental or social problems or collapse. Motivation (energy, empowerment) of the student for every further action in the interests of a human future appears from the results of past actions. The visibility of these results enhances caring for the future.

Self-evaluation of the sustainability of one's habits and lifestyle forms gradually, step by step. The steps constitute educational cycles within topics:
- *Benchmark of starting conditions - first changes*
- *Information search*
- *Formulating intentions, setting goals (what we want to achieve)*
- *Formulating an action plan*

- *Action implementation*
- *Measurements of changes (end-of-program conditions)*
- *Reflection upon the results, self-assessment of actions*

In such a pedagogical system the teacher should be able to listen to the student, to hear him/her and to support his/her self-assessment in the light of general sustainability principles. The teacher does not offer assessments, but invites the students to research, act, and reflect.

The teacher as coach and guide

Educational theory based on empowerment is distinguished by the fact that the teacher is focused not on teaching but on creating the conditions for learning (which gives students an opportunity for self-study and personal development), motivating students, inspiring and strengthening them. The teacher acts more as a coach, i.e. a guide for pupils to find their own solutions, improve performance, learn and develop their skills (ref Myles Downey).

Nowadays, the term coaching is understood as an effective psychological means to enhance personal effectiveness. It is widely used in the field of human resource management. The term "coaching" is used both in sport (to refer to individual and team psychological coaching and consulting), and in management, as a particular leadership style and a form of individual and group counselling.

Using coaching principles and techniques, the teacher helps the students to learn more effectively, to fulfil their personal potential in learning, to change themselves and their lives in accordance with sustainable development goals. The task of the teacher as a coach is to help the student find the resources which s/he needs at the moment and to use them in practice. Coaching boosts self-development, changing the learning process into a "self-improvement" process.

To truly understand the role of a coach, the teacher needs to keep in mind certain features of the learning process in terms of empowerment.

First of all, the student is a 'subject' credited with acting as a conscious and responsible person. Coaching helps broaden an understanding of reality while analysing the set task. The student collects and analyses the information needed to solve educational tasks; the teacher-coach has only a supporting role.

Awareness helps to take responsibility for actions. Students take responsibility for what happens in their lives and become less likely to view themselves as victims of circumstance. In other words, a pedagogy of empowerment intrinsically implies the idea of self-determination, inculcating an attitude towards oneself and the world that supports an active self-identification process. Taking into account the fact that a personality is a complex system functioning at different levels, the student's achievement of even small personal goals in the learning process affects other spheres of her/his life. Positive results in one area of life lead to achievements in others.

In the process of empowering learning, the teacher neither evaluates, gives advice or solutions, nor (ideally!) projects personal experience. The student makes his/her own decisions regarding the steps to her/his goal, and takes personal responsibility for the results. The teacher's task is to help students choose such steps on the way to the goal that each step would be in the "comfort zone" (White, 2009).

To create communicative cooperation and build a partnership between the teacher-coach and the student, it is important for young people to participate in the decision-making process regarding their education and actions, to be given greater power and possibility to really influence the educational process and their own lives, and to make conscious changes. This is only possible with a dialogue, the free and equal discussion of opinions and suggestions, and with cooperation, the combined participation of children, young people and adults in developing mutual projects.

Children, when well informed, have a very realistic view of things happening around them. By taking part in such dialogue, they learn how to communicate with each other, how to discuss and debate, defend their opinions and listen to those of other people. But the most important thing is that they get a chance to really make decisions concerning the issues that affect or concern them.

Thus, empowering teaching is always directed at capacity strengthening and self-actualization. This learning model may bring joy and satisfaction to the teacher, because it is a great happiness to help a child or a group of children realize their potential and abilities and help them understand they are capable of more, and that they received and created it by themselves…

> 66 *The range of what we think and do is limited by what we fail to notice. And because we fail to notice that we fail to notice, there is little we can do to change; until we notice how failing to notice shapes our thoughts and deeds."*
> — DANIEL GOLEMAN ((1985) BOOK VITAL LIES, SIMPLE TRUTHS)

3. AN EMERGING PEDAGOGY FOR ESD

Perspective on learners and learning

Marilyn:
In the first half of the 20th century there was still some debate about the teacher's view of the student. In terms already established in ancient Greece: is the student an empty vessel to be filled, or a fire to be lit?

Clearly in the industrial era the role of schools and teaching had been to produce 'human resources' for the workplace.

> 66 *From an historical point of view education has been torn by a tension rooted in conflicting purposes ascribed to it. This tension lies in the double heritage of humanist and techno-cratic thinking that has shaped the last 150 years of educational thought and practice. Humanism has brought to education a clear vision of academic excellence and the belief that human-ity can transcend their limitations though rationality and the de-mystification of the world. The technocratic approach to learning has seen education as a systems problem in which we need to manage information and bodies in a way that produces a quality human product (the citizen/worker) to maintain and further the values of western capitalist society." —* MARCUS BUSSEY
> (MARCUS BUSSEY IS AN AUSTRALIAN DOCTOR OF PEDAGOGY WHOSE THESIS IS
> BASED ON A NEOHUMANISTIC APPROACH TO EDUCATION.)

While this approach has meant, for the privileged few, a high-quality education as engineers, economists and other specialists, for most people it unequivocally meant 'filling an empty vessel': helping or persuading pupils to accumulate ready-made knowledge deemed to turn them into useful workers. It also meant, quite often, discouraging them from learning 'too much' about topics they were pre-sumed not to need. This was particularly the case with women, who - even in the upper echelons of society - were assumed to take harm from 'too much' knowledge of almost any kind.

A major, but not uncontroversial, ambition of education in Swedish 'third way' socialism, as it began to take shape even before World War II, was to educate people not to fit, but to change existing society: to light social fires, so that many individ-uals would be collectively motivated to bring about a transformation of Swedish society; which indeed took place.

In the new, modern or even post-modern world, a radical shift has taken place. Fire-lighting is still acclaimed as the paradigm - but the fires to be lit are assumed to be individual rather than collective. Students are to be helped to find their own passion, and thus inter alia to participate in designing their own education. A huge bouquet of schools and methods has emerged, with the ambition to enable or empower students: to light their fires. So, it seems, the educational paradigm has taken a turn around a closed circle. High-quality education becomes once again a question of privilege for the few with the opportunity to locate the 'right' schools and make the 'right' personal choices that enable them to benefit from existing social structures.

This educational paradigm works directly counter to the needs of ESD, which brings with it a new educational imperative similar to that faced by Swedish reformers in the mid 20th century: to light social fires, so that many individuals will be collectively motivated to bring about a new transformation. And this new transformation is greater than even those 20th century educational pioneers could dream of.

Because of the enormity of the challenge, it also introduces a new factor: that the teachers are ignorant. Not, of course, in a general sense – but there is no way they (we) can guide students to a 'correct' or 'good' syllabus for sustainable development unless they (we) are also open to the concept that each and every student may have something unique to contribute; something of which the teacher simply cannot conceive.

No longer a vessel, empty or otherwise, or even a fire waiting to be lit; but a unique spirit to be cherished both for itself, and for its potential contribution to the collective issue of sustainable development.

'I don't teach – I facilitate learning,' said an indignant voice at a recent international ESD conference.

Yes indeed. And not any kind of learning, either. Just as earlier generations of students were equipped to take their place in industrial society, so the new generations need to be equipped to co-create a sustainable human society.

Olena:

The Greek saying that a student is not a vessel to be filled, but a fire to be lit became popular in the USSR in the 1980s and 90s due to the prevalence of the so-called "pedagogy of cooperation", which implied a significant increase in student participation in learning, and the establishment of more democratic relations between teacher and students. Compared to the previous authoritarian pedagogy and the slogan "More knowledge and skills to pupils!" it was an important step towards the humanization of the education system. Today, we still can find it on the pages of pedagogical publications or in speeches of teachers in post-Soviet cultures.

I first heard this expression at a lecture for young teachers about thirty years ago.

The question seemed largely rhetorical. However, I have been pondering over it for a long time since both the first and the second part of it came to seem unconvincing.

Regarding filling students' heads with ready-made knowledge, answers and dogmas, it was clear from the very beginning: in such a manner, at best, you will raise a good performer and an obedient person who likes acting only in accordance with clear instructions.

In the era of Soviet industrial development, strengthened by authoritarianism, schools and education in general were required to create "human resources" for enterprises. This is what was meant by filling the "empty vessel". Teachers might either help the pupils accumulate ready knowledge or convince them of the necessity of accumulating it. Often, as in Sweden, it meant also that pupils were warned off topics they "would not need in the future".

However, for me the fire-lighting did not excite positive emotions either. Somehow it made me think of Danko, the character in the story by Maxim Gorky who tore out his own heart and turned it into a torch to lead the foolish people. The people he tried to save did not appreciate his sacrifice. The story had many details I did not like: the silliness of people who could only be impressed by a victim, and the necessity of death for the sake of ideas. Later, both in literature and in real life, I have seen many examples of how foolish or deluded people mindlessly followed the ideas and dictates of self-appointed teachers or gurus.

The idea of education in which the student and the teacher are equally important, and in which "vessels" and "torches" disappear, seems much more productive for me as it reveals huge resources for the personal development of both.

FEAR AND LOVE

A postulate of some spiritually-based pedagogies is that a person can act from two positions only: either love or fear.

Acting from love, we accept ourselves, other people and the world as they are, we trust ourselves, people and the universe, we are full of strength and readiness to understand and support others. Living from love, we are calm, joyful, energetic, and optimistic.

When we act from fear, we are afraid of ourselves ("I won't have enough power, I may be aggressive, I may fall sick…"), of other people ("they don't love or understand me, they won't cooperate with me…"), of the universe ("the world is unfair and dangerous, it has no good place for me…").

This postulate fully applies to the teacher as a person. Several generations of Soviet citizens were educated to fear, and it keeps breeding residual stereotypes and negative programs in people's consciousness. Most often, they provoke authoritarian, non-democratic behaviour of managers towards employees, parents towards children, teachers towards pupils.

A key component is trust:

- *Trusting yourself as the teacher: "My pupils recognize me as the teacher, they need my support and are open for productive cooperation with me and their class-mates. I can always find a way to establish contact and mutual understanding with my pupils."*
- *Trusting pupils: "My pupils are willing to learn life skills and are capable of dis-covering their own learning style, if necessary with my help. They all would prefer to express themselves in kind thoughts and deeds, and all of them have the inner capacity to do it."*
- *Trusting the universe: "Life will always help me to solve difficult problems in the most suitable way for me. It protects me, and any mistakes and hardships are les-sons I could learn from."*

Such a way of thinking and acting is one of the most important challenges in ESD. Without it, there is only a limited possibility to spread SD.

This is an invitation to school curriculum developers to think about introducing into teacher training a special section on developing their ability to trust, as a core characteristic of personal and professional growth in ESD.

CASE STUDY: 'NEOHUMANIST' TEACHING

DADA SHAMBHUSHIVANAND
HTTP://NHE.GURUKUL.EDU/

MARCUS BUSSEY
HTTP://WWW.USC.EDU.AU/UNIVERSITY/FACULTIES-AND-DIVISIONS/FACULTY-OF-ARTS-AND-BUSINESS/STAFF/018555.HTM

Neohumanism is an example of a teaching tradition, practiced in schools in over 50 countries, that consistently puts the student's whole person at the centre of the educational process. As such, it has a significant contribution to make to our under-standing of ESD. The notes below were contributed by Marcus Bussey.

The route to sustainable education lies through an appreci-ation of sustainability at many layers of human action. No one layer can be said to have priority over another, being intercon-nected in an ecology of being that only in its entirety can be said to be sustainable. This is true because sustainability in any limited sense can only ever equal stasis, which ultimately leads to stagnancy. Physical and intellectual sustainability are needed to organise human activity, ethical and emotional sustainability

are required to give this activity coherence, while spiritual sustainability is needed to give the whole process purpose and direction, making it progressive and dynamic.

Neohumanist teaching conveys a sense of rightness and joy to the hearts and minds of children by linking tradition, continuity and change as meaningful and sustainable engagement with life.

Thus living becomes an aesthetic expression of human potential. The founder of neo-humanism, P. R. Sarkar, emphasised the importance of aesthetic science both as a measure of our humanity and as a force taking us ever deeper into the spiritual core of our being. Aesthetics describes relationship, lying at the heart of culture it is the outward expression of our humanity. Thus to take the measure of someone, or a society, we must look at their actions. Sarkar observed that, "the quintessence of aesthetic science is to get joy and give joy." As we all proceed through life we need to use this as a measure of our own success as teachers.

A life without joy is one of quiet desperation. It is ultimately unsustainable. To be a neohumanist teacher is to engage with sustainable activity joyously and to energetically draw others onto the same path.

The personal journey of each teacher

Marilyn:

The observation about balancing hopes and fears (above, An emerging pedagogy) should not be interpreted to mean that only a teacher who is without fear is able to teach SD. Indeed, it's fortunately not a question of being without fear, but rather of what we do with our fears.

A person who is never afraid of anything is probably either very, very lucky, or dead. There is nothing wrong with fears, unless they are allowed to dictate our actions. We can experience a fear, take note of any rational risk - and still choose to act from the place of love inside us.

Learning to do this is truly 'life-long learning'. A teachers' training course incorporating these elements is to be heartily wished for. And… it can only be the beginning, because you cannot teach someone to 'trust', just as you cannot command them to 'respect' another. What can be done is to open the door to these possibilities: an important step in empowerment.

After that, we need indeed to trust that the teachers for whom the door has been opened will find their own ways to neutralize the toxins of fear and mistrust, in their classrooms and in their lives.

> 66 *Feelings are much like waves, we can't stop them from coming but we can choose which one to surf."* — JONATAN MARTENSSON

> 66 *The caricature of the burnt-out teacher living a half-life of frustration and cynicism needs to be thrown out. To teach is the central expression of our humanity. Schooling has formalised this process but it has not altered the fact that people teach people and that children look to their elders to be guided into life. The source of inspiration in teaching is the teacher's joy in living."* — MARCUS BUSSEY

Olena:

The search for effective pedagogical theory and practice for Sustainable Development (ESD) is an on-going path of discovery that more and more people join today. Like sustainable development itself, it is a serious challenge and a great adventure.

In some ways this search combines the challenges facing educators in many countries, such as: equal access to quality education, increased activity and responsibility of students for the results of their learning, lifelong learning, competence development, etc. However, there are also challenges in ESD pedagogy that have not previously been encountered, and issues not yet generally considered.

First of all, the key issue and major discovery in each training program for ESD is the selection and design of learning content: what a person (young or adult) should be taught so that her/his life style would comply with SD. What curriculum content can lead to development of a "sustainable" awareness of how we should live, how to view life, what to strive for and how to evaluate our actions and the actions of others? How much and what kind of information is necessary and sufficient so that the life of our student would keep travelling on "a journey to sustainability" even after their education?

The second question (no matter how worn it may sound!) will be "how to teach". Or rather, how to make our students want, strive for sustainable lives, and learn even without our participation, not only in the classroom or seminar, but in the family, in the street or in their community. What methods, forms of teaching may be employed, what conditions may be created in order to bring about the motivation of students, with real, measurable changes in their lives and behaviour as a result?

Few educational theories can provide answers to these questions. However, the most interesting ideas about effective education we have today can give us some elements, tips, starting points for designing a new type of pedagogy. In this case, the intriguing aspect of the pedagogical search of ESD is in the fact that it is developing in many countries that are often worlds apart. It means that the ESD model which is "transparent" and "successful" in one country always requires new interpretation, serious adaptation and transformation when moving to another country.

And another thought: those who really want to develop the theory and practice of ESD taking active part in this exciting process should always be open to new views, ideas and discoveries - large and small - knowing that we want to teach for a future about which we know little. In this journey of pedagogical discoveries, our colleagues and advisers are both professional teachers and parents of students, the students themselves, and just active people of many professions and ages.

Therefore, although the readers of this book are offered information on experience accumulated in different countries and by different communities of teachers, the use of this experience, its adaptation to the needs of a specific target group of students will certainly still be an exciting adventure, leaving much for your own creativity and discoveries.

COMPONENTS OF ESD

An international workshop in November 2009 explored the question of an appropriate pedagogy for education for sustainable development. Some the major conclusions, formulated in cooperation with Frans Lenglet and Clayton White, were the following.

Two principal components of ESD are transformation and action competence.

Transformation refers to the profound change in the ways in which people and communities, locally and globally, use the planet's biophysical and ecological resources and relate to each other, in view of sustaining the earth's carrying capacity and creating conditions for people to shape their lives and future in terms of social and economic justice and prosperity.

Action competence refers to the intellectual, practical and life skills of learners to comprehend their world in its complexity and to contribute to the necessary collective and individual action required for transformation to occur and be effective.

In this perspective, pedagogy for sustainable development (PSD) transcends the theories, methods and tools that can assist in creating awareness about the unsustainability of certain ecological, economic and social processes, and the role of individual and collective behaviour.

In fact, PSD needs to allow learners to delve into those processes in order to scientifically analyze and understand their physical, biological, ecological, histori-cal, social, economic and political characteristics, drivers and constraints. In addi-tion, PSD assists learners to analyze and comprehend how their own actions and behaviour may be influenced by, may contribute to or may alter these processes, whether positively or negatively.

And it does not stop there. Knowing the ability of individuals and groups to main-tain and psychologically reconcile seemingly internally contradictory behaviour, PSD helps learners to detect the mental patterns (world-views, beliefs, myths, unchallenged mental habits) that underlie, influence or dictate behaviour, even if it is contradicted by the facts or expert opinion. Recognition and understanding of these patterns are a necessary but not sufficient component of the individual and collective action competence, for which PSD also provides the approaches, methods and tools.

From the above, it is clear that conventional and even less conventional pedago-gies fall short of the needs. There are three components or patterns that even now are discernible:

- *Educators need to be enabled to 'release' the role of expert, and to accept that students not only may but shall overtake them, shall create solutions and indeed knowledge of which the educator did not dream. The major role of the educator becomes to liberate the creativity and drive of the students.*
- *Consequently, the view of the student or pupil needs to be transformed. No longer either a 'vessel to be filled' or a 'fire to be lit', the student needs to be seen as a unique spirit to be cherished for its own sake, as well as for its potential contribution to SD – see more under 'Perspective on learners and learning'.*
- *In this liberation of intellect and creativity, the student needs to be enabled to see her or his role as part of the human community. The unique contribution of each indi-vidual to the whole is in focus, rather than the uniqueness of the individual as such.*

Teacher's competencies

To the above we could add that ESD is necessarily multi-modal, engaging as many of the senses and 'intelligences' as possible and flowing in response to the needs of both students and teachers between creativity, hands-on experience, teaching and learning.

After the 2009 workshop, we went on to identify four principles that represent a preliminary response to one of the recurring questions:

What competencies are needed by an SD teacher?

PRINCIPLE 1: REFLECTION IS AN IMPORTANT LEARNING TOOL FOR ESD

Reflection is probably the single most important learning tool for SD. Teachers need the skills to do their own reflection regularly, and to organize the reflective process for their students. In particular they need to be able to formulate questions that stimulate reflection. One example from the workshop was the reiteration of the question 'In what way is this a problem for you…?'.

PRINCIPLE 2: ESD HAS A DYNAMIC FLOW

The work of the students needs to flow from individual to small-group to plenary work, and back to individual reflection. It will also, though this was not specifically elicited at the workshop, necessarily be multi-modal, engaging as many of the senses and 'intelligences' as possible and flowing in response to the needs of both students and teachers between creativity, hands-on experience, teaching and learning. The teacher needs to be able to orchestrate this flow and build bridges between the successive elements.

PRINCIPLE 3: FEEDBACK HAS A KEY ROLE

Teachers need a number of feedback skills. They need to
- *Organize the feedback process for students, quantitatively (measurements, benchmarking) and qualitatively, e.g. individual personal feedback between students.*
- *Give and receive qualitative feedback.*
- *Teach students how to ask for, receive, and give qualitative feedback.*

Asking for feedback includes such skills as creating a brief factual description of the situation/case, analysing strong and weak points, and formulating specific questions.

Receiving feedback includes an ability to receive constructive criticism without feeling personally attacked; and to distinguish between fact, theory, and feelings on the part of the person giving feedback.

Giving feedback includes the ability to listen attentively and non-judgmentally, and to distinguish between fact, theory, and feelings – one's own, and those of the feedback recipient.

PRINCIPLE 4: FOCUS ON THE EXPERIENCE OF STUDENTS

A key skill of the teacher is to facilitate the process of transforming experience into learning. Actual experience is the focus, not knowledge in the conventional sense. The teacher's process consists in repeatedly inviting, and asking, empowering questions. Trust is essential: trust in the students, their experience, and the process.

In addition, our own reflection is that these four areas of competence are useful not only for teachers but also for everyone involved in contributing to sustainable development.

OBSERVATION CONCERNING INDIVIDUAL AND GROUP CHANGE PROCESSES

It has been said that change is not something that can be planned, but rather is something that happens when the conditions are right: when there is a reasonable balance between hope, on the one hand; and dissatisfaction or fear, on the other. (Ziegler, 1995) Since ESD is intended to lead to change, the learning process needs to observe this balance.

The first opportunity comes during the primary analysis. For example, in preparation for the international workshop mentioned above, participants were asked to identify both the things they were most satisfied with, and those they most wished could have been different. Evaluation needs to focus on positive aspects with clarity (not only general congratulation), and on dissatisfaction with courage. Only then can a synthesis be created with the potential to stimulate change.

Olena:
Reflecting on the competencies needed for the SD teacher, it is easy to see, among other things, one fundamentally new feature of the learning process: it seems to play down, almost ignore the importance of the teacher's role. Though, in fact, this is not true. The teacher together with the student remains the key player in the process, but her/his role becomes completely different. True, there is no single solution that would guarantee the successful learning of each student for sustainable development in any situation or context. However, some characteristics of the new teachers who could ensure a consistent positive impact on the learning process have emerged.

International teaching experience shows that students learn better if teachers:

- *Create a supportive learning environment*
- *Develop students' reflective thinking and their activity*
- *Motivate students' learning and mastering new knowledge*
- *Organize interactive learning for students*
- *Establish the relationship between students' acquired knowledge and their experience*
- *Maintain the link between the learning and teaching processes.*

Let us look more closely at these aspects of teacher competence.

CREATING A SUPPORTIVE LEARNING ENVIRONMENT

Education cannot be independent of the social and cultural context. Students learn better when they feel accepted by the teacher, when they experience positive relationships with classmates and teachers, when they are able to be active, and when they are known in their own community. The teacher needs to work on positive relationships within the class and to create a favourable, non-discriminatory and mutually supportive atmosphere. The effectiveness of such teaching will be maximal if the teacher keeps the balance, "the triangle rule": for all students three components are equally important: they themselves, the class they study in, and the topic they learn. A violation of this rule leads to a shift of focus to one aspect only and negatively impacts learning. It is also important for children to build good relationships with both the whole school community, and with their own parents – who possess unique knowledge about them and can thus assist in their education.

The competent teacher takes into account the cultural and linguistic diversity of the student community. Together with children, s/he creates an atmosphere within the class using many cultural elements, including the culture of the whole school, all classmates, and the professional culture of the teachers.

Students learn more productively if they know how to "come back" to information and ideas they have discovered, and to consider them objectively, from different perspectives. Reflective learning connects new knowledge with already known things, allowing students to adapt it for their own purposes and transform their ideas into action. At the same time it develops their creativity and their ability to consider facts and ideas critically, and stimulates metacognition: the pupils' ability to consider their own thinking as a process. The teacher may stimulate such thinking by designing tasks and situations that require from students, first of all, the ability to critically evaluate the materials they use, to detect motivation behind the creation or dissemination of information, to track their own progress and evaluate the results.

MOTIVATION FOR STUDYING

Students learn better when they understand what they learn, why (for what reason) they need to learn this, and how they can use their new knowledge and skills. The competent teacher stimulates the interest of the students, invites them to seek reliable information and ideas, to use knowledge, to try to apply what they have learned in a new context or in a new way. Such a teacher also tries to involve students directly in the process of solving problems connected with their learning, supports their attempts to evaluate their own work, to choose the best methods and ways of learning, and to find the most important meanings for themselves.

ORGANIZATION AND SUPPORT OF TEAM LEARNING

Students learn better when they are involved in a group activity and communication with other people, including peers, members of their own family, those close to them. The teacher supports such cooperation by cultivating a community of learners in the classroom. In such a community everyone, including the teacher, is involved in an educational dialogue and partnership. In this way, support and feedback are always reliable and available. Involvement of students in reflective discourse with others allows them to build the language they need for further learning.

CREATING LINKS BETWEEN NEW AND PREVIOUS EXPERIENCE

Education is always more effective if it gives students an opportunity to integrate new knowledge with existing knowledge. When the teacher consciously links new content with what students already know and are able to do, it saves learning time, meets student needs and expectations, and helps avoid unnecessary duplication of educational content. The competent teacher helps students to establish links between various subjects and branches of knowledge, as well as between their own life practice and the practice of humankind, thus providing ample opportunity to learn.

TEACHER'S SELF-IMPROVEMENT

Since any educational strategy works differently in different contexts and with different students, competent teaching requires from the teacher a constant assessment of her/his impact on students and contribution to their achievements.

Investigation of links between the teacher's own manner of teaching and the learning process for the students is a cyclical, long-term process that happens all

the time, day after day. In this process the teacher asks her(him)self the following questions:

- *What is the focus of teaching in this particular topic and particularly today? What important material (and hence so important that we should spend time on it) shall I give to my students at this lesson and for this topic? Such reflections on the focus of learning give core principles and a common direction. However, the teacher still needs to have precise information about what students already know and what they still need to learn.*

- *What strategies (taking into account the real classroom situation and the real possibilities and needs of these children) can help my students to learn this material in the best possible way? Trying to answer this question, the teacher can focus not only on advanced technologies, methods described in literature or own educational experience, but also on how his/her colleagues organize a learning process in this or another class, given the educational abilities of students to achieve the results the teacher planned in answer to the first question.*

- *What can be considered the result of teaching, and what is the task for the next stage? Reflecting on this question, the teacher should take into account the level of students' results in the light of the planned focus of study. Such an analysis is needed for the teacher in order to assess progress as well as to build a sequence of steps that can reach desired results. An analysis and interpretation of information will help to determine what to do next.*

Action learning, action research

If we are to create a pedagogy and educational approaches that truly meet the needs of sustainable development, then we need to finds way to promote learning that is both individual and collective.

In this, we can learn from methods and approaches developed within what is generally known as action research, and particularly the type of action research sometimes referred to as 'community-based research'. One effective tool is the concept of the audit. In our view all learning for sustainable development should include regular audits, so that we accumulate over time - individually and collectively - a precious data resource to help us research our own needs and opportunities.

There seems at times to be some fuzziness between action research and Action Learning. A useful distinction is that action learning is something you do for yourself: I learn through action/experience, and through seeing the results of my actions. Action research, on the other hand, is (also) concerned with learning for the benefit of others. The experience and results must be replicable and transferable (offered, taught) to others not part of the original practitioner population.

ACTION LEARNING

At the first stage of this kind of learning, the students either actualize their particular personal, academic or life experience and share it among themselves, or, even more likely, acquire this experience through specially organized interaction during the educational activity. The objective here is to search for something new that is worth working with; to search for it in life experience, views, basic knowledge, practice or activity during the lesson (for instance through independent research of people's lifestyle – audit, situation modelling, role play, imitation, experimentation, etc.). The result is the creation of a shared field, as the primary product of students' interaction during their exchange of information and experiences, where further active work will take place.

At the second stage of learning – the stage of reflective thinking – conditions are created for critical understanding and reflection on the experience received by students (or the one they already have), including discussion of observations relating to the process. The main issues discussed at this stage are: "What have we achieved? What was happening during this process? What have we planned and actually achieved?" These questions give rise to new ones that are no longer reflective but conceptualized.

The third stage of learning is a search for information, and its comprehension. It is this stage that allows constructing, building up, and giving students new knowledge and skills. Students look for a bridge from real life situations to generalized conclusions and laws. The effectiveness of this process is improved by the interaction of students, i.e. their overall progress in order to realize their own needs. At this stage, the results of the interaction come in the form of conclusions based on mutual reflection, general arguments, exchange of ideas, and meanings.

As a result of collective thinking, there arises unique knowledge the value of which is not informative in its content, but creative in its nature, because it is always subjectively new for students.

In addition, as one of the ways to explain their experience, at this stage students may also be offered theories or models: theoretical propositions that explain the issues discussed. However, this does not mean replacing personal conclusions by "alien" concepts. The suggested theories should support students to better understand and clarify their own experience.

At the final stage – the stage of "active steps" – the opportunity to check students' conclusions is particularly important: the return from abstract theory to experience. This check occurs in the process of relevant practice, and finally leads to the acquisition of new concrete experience as well as behavioural and activity models, and becomes a new cycle of learning. This can be accomplished, for example, by setting new objectives and planning new actions by students.

Hence, the essence of the new paradigm of education lies in the fact that the educational process is carried out only through the constant activity and interaction of all students. This is interactive, mutual learning where both the student and the teacher are peer, equal subjects of the educational process, aware of what they do and why they do it, plan their activity and predict its results, and reflect on what they know, are able to do, and may accomplish.

ACTION RESEARCH

Action Research is not a single phenomenon but rather a range of methods and approaches. What they have in common is the convergence of researcher and practitioner: researchers participate – in some measure – in the activity being studied, while practitioners contribute – in some measure – to the research.

In other words, the intention of an action researcher is not only to observe, study and describe but also to influence, change the course of events – and observe and record the results. Similarly, the intention of a practitioner in an action research project is not only to engage in an effective change process but also to learn from the process – and to contribute to an analysis that will permit others to learn from the process, too. One may imagine the scope of Action Research on a scale from R(researcher)-dominated on the left to S(subject)-dominated on the right, where some of the 'stations' might be:

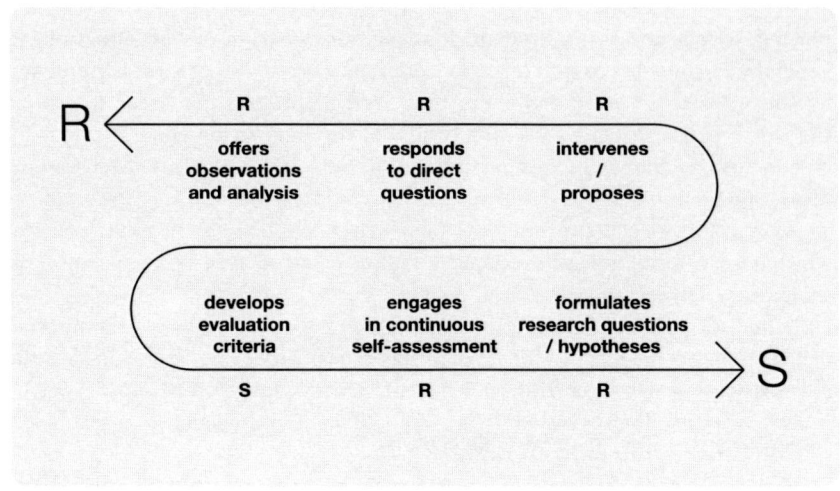

Figure 4. An action research scale

Hart and Bond (1995) identify the essential characteristics of action research as:
- *Educative*
- *Deals with individuals as members of social groups*
- *Problem focused, context-specific and future-oriented*
- *Involves a change intervention*
- *Aims at improvement and involvement*
- *Involves a cyclic process in which research, action and evaluation are interlinked*
- *Founded on a research relationship in which those involved are participants in the change process*

In community-based research, which is on the right-hand end of the scale in Figure 4, the objects of the research have become subjects. This kind of research, and its methods, are available not only to professional researchers but to everyone with a passion to understand. It is one of the foundations of the Learning for Change method described in the chapter on Triple-Loop Learning.

But what KIND of action? What kind of future?

When we talk about taking action, we are talking about change: about the future becoming different from the present, or the future becoming different from what it would have been without our intervention. It is therefore necessary to consider what we know about the future, and how we influence it. A pedagogy for sustainability must of necessity include pictures of the future.

We all – men, women and children – carry within us multiple images of the future. Some are personal, some are collective or cultural, while some may be 'absorbed' from public predictions or prophesies. The images held by any one individual may well be in mutual contradiction to each other; indeed, they often are. (ref Ferucci)

Methods for working with futures – for instance, 'futures studies' – range from the mathematical to the spiritual. For instance, the multitude of current scenarios concerning global climate change are primarily scientific and mathematical. They aggregate what very large numbers of experts believe is likely to happen, under given circumstances.

Such scenarios do not of themselves lead to action, as international affairs eloquently testify. They are however one part of the puzzle that is 'empowerment'. Once people begin to care, once they WISH to take action, no matter whether they are heads of state or schoolchildren, then they need access to reliable information.

On the other hand, our images of the future are what, in the best case, empower us to act and propel us into transformation – both individually and collectively. A noted futurist, Warren Ziegler, said that 'Change is not something we plan. It happens when there is a reasonable balance between dissatisfaction and hope.' In this light, it becomes clear that change is not only or even primarily a rational, intellectual exercise: until feelings and beliefs are engaged, futures work tends to remain sterile. (ref Heath)

To reach the critical balance, we need to work with futures images in several ways:
(ref Inayatullah)
- *To elicit and clarify unarticulated images*
- *To distinguish between images representing hopes, fears, and expectations*
- *To challenge beliefs about what is possible, what is inevitable*
- *To enable dreams to meet and coalesce*

Once the balance is reached, a different kind of on-going futures work is needed to give sustained impetus to the change process.

❝ *The future is a metaphor for the present."* — WARREN ZIEGLER

It is therefore necessary to consider what we know about the future, and how we influence it.

It is easy to fall into the trap of thinking that an education for SD can successfully tell people how to change their behaviour and lifestyles: that there is someone who can tell us 'This is more sustainable, and that is not,' and we have only to transfer this knowledge to our students.

However, trying to influence the future by decree is doomed to fail. Many thinkers have theorized about how the future is created, or co-created, and most agree on at least one thing: that the future is not something we decide or plan; it is what happens when certain conditions are met.

❝ *Change happens when there is a reasonable balance between dissatisfaction (or fear) and hope."* — WARREN ZIEGLER

❝ *Change happens through the tension between what we perceive as 'what is', and what we perceive as 'what could be'."* — ROBERT FRITZ

From this, we can deduce that an important role for educators is to enable students to clarify a number of aspects of their lives:
- *Their hopes and fears*
- *Their perception of current reality*
- *Their expectation of what will happen 'if nothing is done'*

If the objective is only to bring about changes within the current way of thinking, this could be enough to trigger the requisite behaviour changes. But if - as with learning for sustainable development - the objective is to bring about a transformation, then a change of perspective is required. Sustainability is not something we can acquire, buy, learn from a ready-made formula. Solutions developed from this mind-set tend to lack diversity and local relevance (resilience), and will thus themselves prove unsustainable.

We therefore posit the need for an additional component: educators should enable students to step 'outside the box': to gain a broad perspective on what is happening not only in their own lives but also in their surroundings, and thereby to refine or re-define their personal perceptions.

Some of these broader questions are addressed in the chapter 'Educational aspects of sustainability and development'.

4. DESIGNING A PROGRAM OR CURRICULUM

Marilyn:

I see the strong temptation to segment sustainable development into comfortably familiar disciplines, and to teach one thing at a time. A lot of environment, a little democracy, some social integration and new technology – and just possibly, a sprinkle of economics.

Somehow it misses the point. If we improve the environment but go bankrupt, how sustainable is that? If we clean up pollution by introducing dictatorship, how sustainable is that? If we save a lot of money by reducing resource use, and spend it on weapons, how sustainable is that? If we introduce radical and effective political measures towards sustainable development, and get voted out of power before they take effect, how sustainable is that?

No, sustainable development is about transcending boundaries. There are no easy solutions, but somehow we will find ways to work in a transdisciplinary and transsectoral way – scientists, engineers, politicians, business people, activists, economists, municipal planners, philosophers... teachers from all subjects and grades... to enrich each other's ideas about sustainability and challenge our own mental boundaries.

There is also the question of geopolitical boundaries. Sustainability problems are by their very nature global – but solutions are of necessity local. We need to teach in a way that enables us to tackle local issues and concerns within a global context. Making things better for ourselves by making them worse for our neighbours is not too sustainable, either!

And how about cultural boundaries? They may be very obvious, such as groups of people with different languages, lifestyles, dress codes. Or they may be more subtle, as between men and women, adults and children – or teenagers. But one way or another, we are all needed. Everyone has something to contribute.

This is one reason why empowerment is such a key factor in education FOR sustainable development. We need to empower each other to find out what we need to know, and take action accordingly.

Designing an action-oriented program

This section outlines principles for good programs, derived from two decades of experimentation involving hundreds of thousands of people in more than 20 countries; followed by concrete recommendations arising from the principles. It can be used to design a new, action-oriented educational program; or as a checklist to make an existing program even more effective.

The section is by no means definitive. Your contribution can also be valuable. We are all learners, we are all teachers.

Characteristics of empowering programs

The general characteristics of empowering programs, as we have understood them to date, may be summarized in the key principles described below.

1. INVITATION

ESD needs to build on the assumption that the future will bring surprises, new discoveries and opportunities as well as new crises. Therefore, instead of placing all our faith and hopes in existing knowledge, we need to equip our participants with the skills to participate in developing a sustainable future. Only by doing so can we ensure that they will be able to take advantage of opportunities that are beyond the scope not only of our present knowledge, but also of our imagination.

Thus, the goal of ESD is to help every individual to find his or her place in this process, filling him/her with the energy to question behaviour, habits, and lifestyle, assist him/her in helping other people in their development and personal growth.

From this perspective it becomes evident that the teacher's primary role is to create optimal conditions for participants' development, creating and maintaining a climate of safety and creativity in the group. Teaching is no longer a question of giving information: imparting facts or telling what to do or how to do it. Instead, the key task is to awaken the activity of participants, their inner force and motivation for action.

By helping participants along their way, the teacher invites them to act independently in:

- *Setting individual and group goals*
- *Getting personal experience/experimenting*
- *Reflecting*
- *Providing mutual assistance and mutual learning*

So, the teacher invites the participant to act, listens, and is as responsive as possible to his/her needs. The same principle applies to the development of any texts concerning ESD, both for students and teachers. Texts should be innocent of imperatives and orders; their role is to invite the participants to make their own choices based on increasing insight, awareness and discovery.

2. CONTINUITY

Program development is based on several repetitive elements:

- *An ongoing cycle: choice of action and methods → finding out (research/information search) → action+results → reflection*
- *Low threshold, small steps: each participant picks an action to suit him/herself, in order to obtain a measurable or visible result, and works at his/her own pace*
- *Team work: cooperation (including intercultural aspects) is the basic educational model*

3. FOCUS

Clear focus of the curriculum, of the whole learning process, and of each lesson:

- *On individual solutions and the choices of each student, team and teacher*
- *On collective human needs in a planetary context*
- *On leading by example, and helping students to do the same*

4. LEGITIMACY

- *Endorsements*
- *Publicized results*

This principle means that everything that has been done should be made legitimate or, in other words, both acceptable to the primary 'target groups', and – in the case of a school curriculum – also officially adopted for the national educational system. One of the keys is to give wide publicity to practical results.

5. CARING

Caring about something is the basis for motivation for action. Teachers and students care
- *About the program topic, and related concerns*
- *About each other – classmates, team members*
- *About other program participants, eg parents*

Choice of topics and learning material is connected with those aspects of sustainable development that are most relevant and important for the participants in their life today and in the future. On one hand, students are aware of and concerned about certain problems, and on the other, they want to solve them, to believe in their capacity to act effectively. Caring about something creates a basis for action.

During actions students cooperate in teams, exchange opinions and information, support each other and collectively contribute to overcoming any difficulties.

By using the empowerment pedagogy, the teacher demonstrates in action important aspects of caring: care for the students, care for the topic, care for oneself. S/he thus stimulates the activity of students and enhances their levels of caring, creativity and action.

6. FORMULATING QUESTIONS

There is an emphasis on problematique rather than solutions (questions rather than answers). There is an on-going process of asking questions by teachers and participants: questions predominate over answers during the sessions.
- *What is interesting?*
- *What is important?*
- *What do I really need to know in order to take action?*
- *What results have I achieved?*
- *What do these results mean?*
- *What else would I like to do?*

7. AUDITS

Each program or topic begins with personal research: participants explore their own lifestyle and habits, i.e. make audits. The main question every participant has to respond to is "How sustainable are my habits and the lifestyle of my family?"

This research helps them answer the following questions:
- *What choices am I making today, consciously or unconsciously?*
- *Where is my scope for action, my capacity for change?*

As participants work through the program, they continue to formulate questions and need to consider the meta-questions:
- *What else is important to know?*
- *Where to look?*
- *Whom/what do I trust?*

The information search involved in conducting an audit is also a method of going deeper into the topic, becoming more aware of the issue and possible ways of resolving it, also of initiating discussion in teams or groups. Continuing the research opens the space for a gradual understanding that the students' actions will be useful not only for them, but for humanity as a whole. The repeat audit at the end of the topic allows appreciation of the changes that have taken place in the lives of the participants.

8. FORMULATING INTENTION

In psychological theory, intention is a stepping-stone between a wish to change, and the action that will bring about the change (Assagioli, 1974).

On the basis of the audit results, participants are supported to formulate their intention to act, their expectations of the results, and the resources and time needed. The intentions are presented to their teams.
- *I will do this, by that date*
- *I need resources and help/skills*
- *I will know I have succeeded when…*

9. ACTION

- *Try it!*
- *Observing and supporting*

During the sessions, participants are invited to take experimental action. The proposed actions are very simple, for instance: think before buying; try to avoid purchases for at least one day and see what happens. The learning process becomes even more effective when participants are invited to support each other in formulating intentions, acting and observing. This is important not only for the actions themselves, but also for energizing for action, i.e. empowerment.

The teacher, from her/his side, observes the learning process, supporting participants when necessary.

10. FEEDBACK

The learning process provides for regular feedback about participants' actions as well as ideas that they receive from other participants and the teacher. By reflecting upon the results and value of the actions made, we create motivation and empowerment to act in the future. Reflecting on the options for action and on personal results enriches individual experience and improves personal competence.

Feedback is about capturing and evaluating the results of action:
- *This is what happened*
- *How it could have been (even) better*
- *Extrapolation and dissemination*

Since the experience of every participant of SD is unique, it is extremely important to organize an on-going exchange of experience and ideas, as well extrapolation of the results. This is not about competition between participants, or mechanical comparison of the results (whether one did more or less than the other). Cooperation, dialogue and support are keys to ESD, creating an environment in which all results as well as all participants are valued.

The Masters thesis from the UK below (ref Jacometti) is focused on a single, highly topical issue, namely how to bring about energy saving. Its findings support several of the conclusions in this chapter. Several other independent research reports are listed in the references, eg Staats et al, Hargreaves.

CASE: EXCERPT FROM A MASTERS THESIS ON BEHAVIOUR CHANGE

CREATING AND SUSTAINING A BEHAVIOURAL CHANGE IN ENERGY CONSERVATION

Excerpted from a Masters thesis by Stéphanie A. Jacometti, London, 2009

INTRODUCTION

In the last thirty years, energy efficiency and energy conservation have been seen as increasingly important. Campaigns seeking to address demand have so far concentrated on raising awareness and providing information, but this has not changed behaviour significantly. For example, the UK Government has tried to change behaviour by taking a generalised, mass-marketing approach which appears to have had little significant impact.

The overall aim of this thesis was to analyse what elements of a programme could change energy-using behaviour in the long term, and for instance to understand the behavioural change process, and why people change their behaviour.

THE BEHAVIOURAL CHANGE PROCESS AND CAMPAIGNS

The research reviewed shows that providing information and changing attitudes will most likely not lead to a change in behaviour. Behaviour change campaigns are more resource intensive than awareness-raising campaigns, but are more effective.

Several factors have been shown to be effective in encouraging people to change their behaviour. These include feedback, prompts, personalised advice and collective action. Collective action, or community support, is especially important when people learn that others are doing their bit and, as a result, may want to emulate those in their direct environment.

The programs run by an NGO, Global Action Plan, integrate a number of these factors, such as a group setting, material, and feedback in the form of measuring and monitoring. Rather than discussing radical measures to save energy, the programs focus on no- or low-cost practices, which can become habits and - eventually - routines.

RESULTS

When asked what key lessons they learned during the design, implementation and evaluation of their programmes, interviewees said it was important to engage with partners, and to have a very specific aim. For the evaluation stage, the following methods to gauge the outcomes were mentioned: CO_2 as a measurement, qualitative data, external evaluators, and feedback in the form of surveys filled out by participants.

In order to complement behavioural change programmes, a number of interviewees suggested rewarding good behaviour by investing in something that would benefit the whole community, such as a park. It was also felt that energy advice services should be personalised so that individuals would not be burdened with excess and unwanted information.

CONCLUSIONS

The following conclusions can be drawn from the primary and secondary data.
- *Distinguish between advice and information. Advice is personalised, whereas information is of a more general nature.*

- *Both the message and the messenger are important; the message should be clear and consistent, and ideally should come from a trusted source such as friends or family.*
- *Providing feedback and focusing on communities were identified as important success factors.*
- *A forum is needed to bring all the stakeholders together, so that there is an opportunity to collaborate. This would also increase the likelihood that the message sent to individuals is consistent.*
- *School education was seen as important so that young people can grow up with energy conservation, while becoming more environmentally aware.*
- *It is important to work simultaneously on policy and behaviour, i.e. top-down as well as bottom-up.*
- *NGOs are well positioned to achieve changes in the ways in which we use energy since they can take more risks over longer timescales than government initiatives. However, NGOs find it difficult to select the most effective programmes.*

RECOMMENDATIONS

Several recommendations can be made from the research, including the following.

1. National campaigns usually last a short period of time and are often ineffective in changing behaviour. The community-focused Global Action Plan programs last for several months and are carried out on a smaller scale, but have been proven to be effective. A far-reaching campaign should probably last a number of years using multiple communication channels, including media and one-to-one approaches.

2. Evaluating a programme in order to gauge its effectiveness is very important but is often not carried out thoroughly.

- *The Global Action Plan programs are an exception, with numerous studies focussing on their outcomes.*
- *Funds are often available for quantitative analysis but not qualitative, as the latter is more resource intensive. It would however make it easier to determine which programmes are demonstrably successful in changing behaviour.*

Invitation to action

An ESD program needs to invite action. The invitation needs to be specific, concrete, and easy to understand.

This requirement could be in conflict with the basic principle of empowerment, i.e. that each person brings his or her own experience and circumstances to the process of sustainable development. It is thus important to see, develop and present the specific invitations as a kind of 'starter kit' - not a final blueprint, but a possible way to experiment with new daily habits. In such a context, the invitation becomes one element of the spiral of empowerment.

But which invitations are appropriate? The world is full of books offering a hundred (or even a thousand) ways to save the world. Rigorous selection can reduce the number, but still the invitations will be sufficiently many to need some kind of structure.

Sometimes the curriculum design process begins with choosing a set of topics and then selecting appropriate actions; sometimes with choosing a set of actions and then grouping them into appropriate topics. We have found no general rule for this; it depends on the circumstances, for instance the priorities of principals.

CHOOSING TOPICS

A basic principle is to group actions into topics that have relevance for participants. It is for example NOT usually helpful to use abstract categories - like for instance the classical elements of earth, air, fire, water (and in some traditions, spirit). The closer you come to the daily lives of the participants, the easier your pedagogical task will be.

In Global Action Plan programs the topics of garbage and energy are given, though in some countries energy is split into different categories: travel, electricity, home heating and cooling… In most countries water is also an obvious topic - not necessarily in Iceland or Norway, though, where it may not be easily understood that water is something in need of care and attention.

Other frequent topics are buying habits and eating habits, as well as different aspects of care for the natural environment. Coming up strongly are such topics as personal relations, group dynamics and participative democracy, care for one's own health, responses to economic crises.

In work places, purchasing criteria can come into focus and specific raw materials may also become topics of their own. For example, paper is a common topic in office work places.

DESCRIBING A TOPIC

For each topic, it is useful to emphasize one or more aspects that the participants have a possibility to influence – personally, not only by influencing other people. For example, the social aspect of SD for children of 14-15 years may be described under such headings as Relationships with adults, Family, Our class, Community.

We find it useful to summarize reasons for focusing on the topic in 2–5 short sentences. For instance, the following are the reasons offered for choosing Personal Relations as a topic for Ukrainian teenagers:

- *People themselves are crucial for sustainable development.*
- *One of the basic human needs is a need to communicate.*
- *The success of communication depends on simple but important things that we can learn to do better.*
- *Good relations contribute to good health and healthy development.*
- *Conflicts between humans can trigger violence and even war, and become life-threatening.*

The introductory material to any topic is typically very brief. The main focus is on what is desired (eg clean water, supportive relationships, active trade union members, gender equality etc.). What is not desired – the problematique, or reason for focusing on the topic – is understood through its opposite (eg water pollution, mutual aggression, passivity, discrimination), reinforced by facts/statistics.

An example: the introduction to water from the Ukrainian "Lessons for Sustainable Development" textbook:

You can survive for a couple of weeks without food; but without water, for only 5 days. You need 2.5 litres of clean water a day for drinking.

Consider that if you leave a tap running, 12-20 litres of water may run out in a single minute.

Water cannot be seen as a completely renewable resource. Caring about it is an important part of a sustainable lifestyle. If every citizen of Kiev saved only 1 litre of water a day, the whole city would save 3000 tons of drinking water each day – more than enough to fill an Olympic-size swimming pool.

Using less water, you may also reduce your household expenses for water, sewage and energy.

Some facts:

- *About 71% of the Earth's surface is covered with water, but only 1% of it is usable for drinking, cooking, washing and growing plants.*
- *Everyone who lives in a city uses about 300 litres of water a day: 20% for dish-washing, 20% for bath and shower, 20% for flushing toilets, 15% for laundry. And 15% is lost due to running or dripping taps, 5% used in cooking, and 5% on other activities.*

Get to actions quickly – the time and space given to teaching *about* the topic should be short. It can contain references for those who want to know more.

Make sure that for each topic you have an appropriate number of actions to propose; as a rule of thumb, 6-9 is a good number; and that they represent a reasonable spread of options for your readership. If you find you have many more, consider splitting the topic into two. If you have too few, perhaps there is a natural combination with another topic?

SELECTING INITIAL ACTIONS TO PROPOSE

An empowering program builds on personal choice and personal decisions. It therefore includes options from which participants can select. But this is not about listing everything you can think of: one of the most frequently asked questions is: "Where should I start?" In other words, the number should be possible to grasp and choose from.

For example, on the topic of reducing waste there are actions that fit well with the general principle of 'reduce, re-use, recycle', and are applicable in most countries and for most age groups. In Lessons for SD, for Ukrainian teenagers, they are formulated as follows:
1. Sort garbage for recycling
2. Use recycled paper
3. Compost
4. Use cloth bags for shopping
5. Repair broken items
6. Re-use: The second life of old things
7. Help your community

ASSESSING POSSIBLE ACTIONS

When designing your program, how do you decide which options to offer and which to leave out?

For each topic, it's helpful to offer some quantity options and some quality options. For instance, in the above list one can measure recycled paper use and composting; using cloth bags for shopping instead of plastic bags is a qualitative lifestyle change that can be assessed but not measured.

When choosing actions, one can use the following criteria:
- *There should be a reasonable total number of options; 6-9 per topic seems to be most effective*
- *Each option should be do-able for many. In the example above, all the actions except for 3 and 7 may be immediately implemented by teenagers.*
- *Each option should have a low threshold and/or a step-by-step structure — there should be something participants can do immediately.*
- *Options should be (relatively) uncontroversial (see below)*

CONTROVERSY

If participants run a strong risk of reading or hearing that this option is actually not a good idea — if for example there is a running academic battle about its merits and demerits — then as a general rule, leave it out. If you include it, include information about the battle and say why you chose to include it.

In the Ukraine, for example, public opinion - including doctors - ridicules a vegetarian diet. Therefore we included the following cautious recommendation: "Try replacing at least one meat dish a day by a vegetarian dish; or at least once a week".

FINAL SELECTION

When ranking options against the scales below, choose those which score high on the left-hand side unless there is an exceptionally high pay-off (for the environment, time, money, fun…) to be found on the right.

SIMPLE ⟵⟶ CHALLENGING

FREE ⟵⟶ COST MONEY

HABITUAL ⟵⟶ ONCE-OFF

QUICK ⟵⟶ TIME-CONSUMING

For example:
1. It may be difficult to refrain entirely from sweet things, but participants could be invited to replace candies with dried fruits
2. Buying eco-labelled products may cost more, but the use of local products can help to reduce expenses
3. Weather-stripping windows to prevent draughts costs a little money, but closing the curtains or moving a bed or chair further from the window costs nothing
4. Replacing a single trip to a tourist resort by hiking is less effective than developing a habit of walking to work
5. Turning the taps off when cleaning teeth is an immediate action; buying and installing a water meter takes time and money.

DESCRIBING ACTIONS

Structural and textual focus needs to be on solutions: WHAT can be done, HOW to do it, or find out how to do it, and WHY it is good to do, including 'what's in it for me'. This is described in more detail in the section on 'Audits, media and language'.

Here is an example of the action called "The last one switches off" from "Lessons for SD". The same structure is used for all the actions proposed in the Ukrainian and other textbooks designed according to these principles.

THE LAST ONE SWITCHES OFF

Why should you do this?
Imagine the Earth as your best friend. You can help it every time you leave a room. All you need to do is to switch off electric devices. It will reduce energy consumption and air pollution, and will help your family to save money on electricity.

How to do it
- If you are the last leaving a room, turn the lights off
- When leaving a room, switch off all electrical apparatus - radio, TV, DVD....

What do you need?
The wish to act for sustainable development

Time needed
A couple of seconds

What resources do you save?
You can easily reduce the amount of money your family spends on electricity by 10%. And there's a bonus: every time you reduce electricity use by 1 kWh, you actually save 1.4 kWh, because transmitting the electricity to your house also takes energy.

What do you get?
A new, useful habit.

A good model for such a description is a clear and simple cookbook. The structure, words and pictures combine to create a compelling invitation. The reader should feel that doing the action, if it is at all relevant to her/his situation, would be a) easy, b) fun, c) useful.

For those who are curious about the 'why', it is useful to have references – the text itself should be very short, more to whet the appetite than satisfy it.

Audits

It is a basic human characteristic to notice change, to seek change – and to forget it, once it has happened. (ref Bergson/Protevi) We may complain about change imposed on us by others, but once we are accustomed to it we will probably 'forget' that we did things differently before.

To maintain a development process it is important for participants to be able to track their own progress. This means carrying out audits, whether formal or informal, qualitative or quantitative. It is by recording what happens that we reinforce our will and ability.

MEASUREMENTS

The rationale for quantitative audits at the personal level is the same as for qualitative audits, that is, as a support for personal progress: benchmarking and follow-up.

More credence is often attached to quantitative audits, which means that publicizing them can help give legitimacy to the program. Quantitative results can sometimes also be used (more easily than qualitative audits) as a basis for influencing decision-makers, for instance politicians, municipal planners or business.

To create a quantitative audit:
- *For each topic, look for measurables*
- *Select one or more that meet the criteria (below)*
- *Describe a procedure to carry out measurements*
- *Test the procedure – yourself, and then with 'typical' participants*

In "Lessons for Sustainable Development" most topics include 1-2 measurements. For instance, in the garbage topic students are invited to measure the volume of garbage generated by the family, and the proportion that is recyclable.

The measurements are thus not connected to particular actions; they are linked to the topic as a whole. Some topics do not include measurements, because none are found to match the criteria.

Criteria. An item can be included for measurement if it:
- *Can be measured by most participants*
- *Can be influenced by the participants, individually and/or collectively*
- *Can be measured by a procedure that takes little time and can be experienced as interesting/fun*
- *Is related to long-term change rather than once-off or short-term change*
- *Can (preferably) be shown to change over the period of the program*
- *Is directly/substantially meaningful to the topic*

As an example, we show below the measurement of buying habits used by several programs.

Save all your household receipts for a week. At the end of the week, review the receipts, looking especially for eco-labelling and for locally produced goods. Note your purchases, for example in a table:

Day	Total no. of items bought	Eco-labelled items	Items produced locally	Packaging
1				
2				
3				
4				
5				
6				
7				
Total				

The last column can be used for noting the kind and type of packaging, and numbers of different layers, if one of the action invitations is to reduce the amount of packaging carried home.

QUALITATIVE AUDITS

The easiest kind of audit is qualitative. It is used to "capture" habitual behaviour, and changes to it. Participants are asked to describe certain aspects of their habitual behaviour in order to identify possible changes and set benchmarks. Participants can be offered ready-made forms with a set of statements about the behaviour related to certain actions. Working with the forms, participants may simply note the presence of such habits or describe the frequency of making certain actions, grading from 1 to 5.

Let us consider an example from "Lessons for Sustainable Development". Each question (statement) in the qualitative audit is directly linked to an action that is described in one of the course topics. There are no 'general' questions on the list, i.e. unconnected with specific actions. As a rule, each action has one (occasionally two) corresponding question. Actions are described in the audit as a short statement, e.g. "I switch off lights when there is no one in the room". Below is part of the qualitative audit.

QUESTIONNAIRE

What do my family and I do with garbage?
- *I know which types of wastes can be recycled in my area*   *Yes / No*
- *We sort garbage for recycling*   *1 2 3 4 5*

Saving paper
- *I collect used paper*   *1 2 3 4 5*
- *I save paper by using both sides*   *1 2 3 4 5*

What do I do with organic waste?
- *I know what compost is*   *Yes / No*
- *I know composting rules*   *Yes / No*
- *We compost our organic waste*   *Yes / No*

How do I carry my shopping?
- *I use bags given by the cashier*   *1 2 3 4 5*
- *I carry a cloth bag for shopping*   *1 2 3 4 5*

TO DESIGN A BEHAVIOUR AUDIT

- *List the action options you are proposing*
- *Ask participants to note whether/how often they already do each action, as in the example above*
- *Invite them to set goals for change*
- *Offer them the audit at the beginning of the program, and again at the end, so that they can measure progress*

This is also a very useful exercise to assess how concrete and do-able your action proposals are. If you can't formulate a good question, maybe you should reformulate the action!

There are two kinds of possible replies: binary and proportional. They are expressed like this:
- *I do this action*   *Yes / No*
- *I do this action – seldom / less than half the time / about half / more than half / always*
You may in either case also want to include the option to reply 'not relevant'.

The 'proportional' replies can be treated statistically because they correspond closely to *0% – 25% – 50% – 75% – 100%* in fact, more accurately than if you ask respondents to estimate percentages.

"But this only tells us what people want us to think – not what is really true!"
  This objection to qualitative audits is sometimes heard. It is true that for this reason the results are less important externally, though they are very important 'internally': the personal motivation factor is high. For this reason the questions need careful design so that no respondent should feel they are giving the 'wrong' answer.

It is sometimes claimed that questions should be mixed to reflect desired and undesired behaviour – for example that it should not be obvious that answers on the right are good (more sustainable) and those on the left are bad. This is probably underestimating the respondents, whether adults or children. More important is the review of words to remove those with strong positive or negative associations.

AN AUDIT CAN BE A WHOLE PROGRAM...

It is possible simply to offer participants an audit, usually a qualitative questionnaire. In many cases the very fact of completing a well-designed questionnaire leads to immediate behaviour change.

In other words, the audit is one of the most powerful tools for behaviour change. It can be reinforced, for example by inviting participants to
- *Choose what they would like to change or improve*
- *Fill in a 'pledge form' undertaking certain changes*
- *Fill in the questionnaire again after a certain time*

Some web-based audits make an automatic assessment of the items that would be easiest to change or improve, and generate proposals for simple action programs tailored to the participant.

There is no doubt that the addition of the other pedagogical ingredients described in this book will considerably improve the results, beyond what can be achieved with a simple audit: both as to quantity of results, and their durability over time. But still, the auditing process - an essential component of ESD programs - is in itself possibly the most cost-effective way of achieving small results.

Measuring educational success

When we have created and delivered an ESD program: how do we decide whether or not it was successful? What are the criteria, how can success factors be measured or assessed, how good is 'good enough'?

All formal education systems, and some informal ones, contain some element of assessment or grading of the students. Students' grades are one indicator of the quality of an education program, though not the only one.

In the case of education for sustainable development, student learning should presumably be assessed on the basis of their subsequent actions, rather than on their knowledge.

The first key question would seem to be: Do students in fact take steps to behave more sustainably?

This question underscores the importance of audits, described above. The first reason for including audits is for the benefit of the student; the second is for the benefit of others, such as teachers, who are tracking and aggregating progress.

A second key question: Are the students transformed, at some deeper level, so that in addition to actual, discrete behaviour change they have acquired greater self-knowledge as well as an understanding of the underlying reality of sustainability, namely that everything is connected? Will their learning experience enable them to continue on their own path of sustainable development? And even to influence others?

One dimension of this question is personal maturity. Have the students set foot on a path of personal or spiritual development? Are there any ways to assess this?

A third question concerns the effectiveness of the education. Does it address the groups who will be most effective at disseminating their learning to others? Does it do it with a reasonable input of time, money, and other resources?

There may be good reasons for addressing other groups, or for spending 'unreasonable' amounts of time and money on some of them. But the resources we have available for ESD are tiny in comparison with the size of the task, and we need to husband them.

At the moment we have no indicators for what constitutes a 'reasonable' input of resources. This is an area calling for research.

Audience, media and language

CAN YOU CHOOSE YOUR AUDIENCE?

Perhaps your audience is 'given', as a result of your professional or life situation. Or perhaps you have a choice. Here are some thoughts about choices of audience.

CHANGE AGENTS, EARLY ADOPTERS, OR BOTH?

There may be trade-offs between reaching many people who each do a little, and fewer people who each do more. What is most effective?

According to the theory of social diffusion (ref Atkisson, Rogers), it should best be a combination. The 'few who do a lot' are change agents whose example can, under the right conditions, inspire many others. The results of the 'many who do a little' can on the other hand be useful for wide publicity.

PERSONAL CHANGE – BUT WHICH PERSONS? WHICH ARENA?

ESD programs may be designed to bring about behaviour change by the participants, or to support them to influence other people - for example, by formal lobbying or informal peer pressure; or both.

We believe that effective ESD needs to begin with personal change. Influencing other people is an optional extra. Without the personal change, attempts to 'change' other people have a much smaller chance of success.

Some ESD programs focus on people in a work setting, some on the home and leisure settings. An interesting feature of an empowering program is that, unlike most behaviour-change programs, it is not context-dependent. This means that a person who participates in an empowering program at work or school tends also to change his/her behaviour at home, and vice versa. So the question of choice of arena is not critical. However, more research into relative effectiveness would be useful.

School programs are a good example. For instance, school programs directed primarily to pupils can either focus on helping pupils to improve the sustainability of the school (and thereafter/thereby to influence private and family behaviour patterns); or on private and household behaviour patterns, maybe with an option to continue by working with the sustainability of the school. Which is more effective, under which circumstances? We don't know, yet.

MEDIA, METHODS, PUBLICITY

Traditionally ESD programs make heavy use of written materials (including work-books and audits), teamwork, and team coaching. Experiments with individual rather than team programs have not been an outstanding success, with some exceptions building on mass mailing.

We are also following experiments with other forms, eg
- *Internet as a basis for both individual and group action (see 'Empowerment via the web')*
- *Oral lessons using very little written material*

A project to produce materials in comic book form has been tested by Global Action Plan in Belarus and Kosovo. The idea is to teach participants about both sustainable lifestyle and about how to draw comics - especially wordless comic strips. One objective is to enable exchange of experience between pupils lacking a common language.

Interesting ideas have been broached concerning local radio and TV, but not yet (as far as we know) implemented. CD-roms have been used, sometimes in combination with a 'pledge' form. We are also aware of experiments with games – regular board games. There should be good scope for computer-based games, especially now that they are becoming less expensive to develop.

FEEDBACK SYSTEMS

An essential component of this pedagogical approach is the careful design of information systems for individual and group feedback as well as wider publicity. Because of the innate human capacity to 'forget' change, we need reminding of our progress; successful programs usually include mechanisms for collecting, analysing, and publicizing results.

In particular we recommend that in the first two years of operation, any program is very carefully monitored. This is not only individually empowering, nor only valuable PR material, but is also an important instrument for program improvement. If you compare your results with those of another program, perhaps in another country, you may find ways to get better results - and to help others to do so.

USE OF LANGUAGE AND DESIGN

Regardless of whether texts are for printing, for the web, or for oral presentation, there are some rules of thumb that can be applied to enhance empowerment. The suggestions in this section have been distilled from work with many programs.

CAPTURE THE ESSENCE

There is an adage that when meeting a person or group whom you wish to engage, the first minute is crucial: if in those 60 seconds you attract their attention, awaken their curiosity, then they will be receptive to the rest of your message. This is sometimes called, in American, 'the elevator pitch': a message (pitch) that may engage a person encountered in a lift (elevator). With written material we may have more than 60 seconds, but the principle is the same: opening chapters and paragraphs need to attract, and especially to appeal to the imagination.

At its simplest, it could mean saying something about the audience rather than about ourselves. Too often we begin by talking about what WE think the other person should know, rather than about them and their interests.

In a school setting, we may for instance wish to prepare students to engage their parents in their learning. Each student needs to understand the principle of the 'elevator pitch', and to work on their own message to their parents - written or spoken. The messages can be very different.

For example:
- *We have this new topic in school and I think I could get really good marks, but I'll need some help*
- *You know you've been nagging me about wasting energy? Well, now my teacher's saying the same thing, and I think I'm beginning to get it. Can you help with my homework?*

In any kind of team we can practice our 'elevator pitches' for different audiences - local politicians or journalists, neighbours, colleagues…

FOCUS

Structural and textual focus is on solutions:
1. WHAT can be done
2. HOW to do it, or find out how to do it
3. WHY it is good to do

In relation to sustainable development, the perspective of "why" is on human needs in a planetary context. Sustainable development is not about saving the planet (which doesn't need saving), but saving humans: helping ensure that the planet will continue to be a human habitat.

TEXT

Words and sentence structure should preferably
- *Be invitational, not morally imperative.*
- *Offer choice, not directives*
- *Keep a low threshold. For adult materials this may mean making the text easily accessible to (say) an averagely educated 15-year-old, with implications for vocabulary and sentence structure.*
- *Use technical terms and jargon only when indispensable; explain.*

Below are two examples:
1. An explanation of how and why to fill in a household audit, from a Ukrainian school book
2. An invitation to action from a Hungarian consumer guidebook

AUDIT INSTRUCTIONS

In Lessons for Sustainable Development we will look at daily habits and lifestyle. So it is useful to record your daily habits before we start. We invite you to do this using a special 'audit' questionnaire.

Completing the audit is not a competition. There are no "right" or "wrong" answers - just honest and dishonest. The only person who can fool you - is you yourself! Your answers will remain for as long as they do not need you again.

After learning and taking action, you will come back to these questions. Filling in the audit a second time will help you see what changes you have made. It will be a chance for you and your team to be a little bit proud.

But what if you find no changes? It's never too late to start! Use the opportunity to plan what you'll do the following week or month.

CHOOSE PLANET-FRIENDLY FOOD

WHY ACT?

The food in the shops is usually energy-intensive. Very often, it takes more calories (energy) to produce it than you get from eating it – not a very good bargain, even if it's cheap! It may also be contaminated with chemicals, and it may have been the reason for many other people to suffer. If you eat like an average Hungarian, you can make a huge difference with small changes.

HOW TO DO IT

Decide to eat less meat; for instance
- *Start with one vegetarian instead of meat meal per week, and then evaluate*
- *Reduce the size of the meat portions, adding more vegetables and especially root vegetables*

Check where your food comes from! You may not be able to 'buy local' at all seasons, but you can probably reduce the distance travelled to your table.

Buy food when it is in season close to you, and choose other food in the 'off season'. For instance in winter your salads can contain fewer tomatoes and more root vegetables.

You will need
- *A good vegetarian cookbook, and an hour or so to experiment*
- *A few more minutes in the shop*

The effects
- *Better health, support for local farmers – and a significant decrease in pollution and energy use.*

DESIGN

Feature real people: *Whether written or oral, material benefits from including interviews, experience, anecdotes, photographs.*

Humour: *Humour can be highly empowering!*

Illustrations: *Illustrations (whether photographs, drawings or charts) should have the same focus as the text, i.e. primarily solution-oriented rather than problem-oriented.*

Cultural adaptation

ESD programs built on empowerment principles share several important characteristics. For instance, all of them build on the "empowerment spiral". However, it is clear that implementation of such programs in any country requires cultural adaptation. Attempts to copy a program from one country to another have almost always failed.

We think that it is connected with differences in educational traditions and systems, in lifestyles, habits and ideas of what is "correct" and "incorrect".

Additionally, choice of appropriate actions vary from place to place; exhorting Norwegians to save water can be inappropriate, and suggesting eco-labelled goods, or a choice of electricity from renewable sources, is only appropriate where such choices exist.

In the international Global Action Plan community of organizations we have spent a lot of time developing an adaptation process that allows us to transfer programs - and results - from one country or culture to another. Adaptation of the program starts with adaptation of the educational materials (books and other media) by teams of local experts, who may be teachers, professors, coaches, NGO members. The development teams are first offered training in the principles of empowering design.

Before or during adaptation, the development teams participate personally in the program, so that their adaptation is also based on personal experience. So in addition to their professional expertise their departure points are three:
- *Theories and models received via the workshop*
- *Personal experience*
- *Selected materials from different countries*

The teams then work to select the topics and proposals for action to be offered to participants, and draft workbooks and other materials appropriate to the social and cultural context.

As the materials are developed, national and local data are incorporated: facts, anecdotes, statistics. These increase the participants' interest significantly and enable them to care about resolving personal issues. Using empowering language for writing texts gives an opportunity to include typical metaphors, proverbs and jokes into the material, enriching it with a local flavour.

The final adaptation takes place during a test phase involving considerable feedback and revision of materials. Each test team has a trained coach appropriate to the type of program; they may for instance be leaders of adult study groups, or teachers, or youth leaders.

In our experience cultural adaptation does not happen overnight; it usually takes about a year. This does not mean, however, that no results are obtained for a whole year. Usually the adaptation teams begin to report concrete results within about three months.

Empowerment via the web

Is it possible to produce long-lasting behaviour change through web-based programs? What are the peculiarities of action pedagogy, when the learning is expected to take place via Internet whereas the resulting behaviour change is expected to happen 'in real life'?

EDUCATIONAL SITES

One case is when the learning still clearly takes place within an educational context. Many universities and some schools now use internet-based courses as a staple part of their programs. And many software packages are available to help teachers design and run the courses.

In addition there is a rapid proliferation of sites addressed to the general public with an educational message, often connected to one specific aspect of sustainability: 'save energy' seems to be the current (2012) favourite in the wake of huge publicity about global climate change.

SOCIAL SITES

Another case is when a web site is designed to bring about learning for sustainable development, but profiles itself as a social site rather than an educational site. This is an option that begs to be used when considering reaching large numbers of people.

There are also some mixed solutions, for instance a Norwegian site called 'the climate club' - Klimaklubben, described briefly in the next chapter. It has a clearly pedagogical profile but is designed much like the popular social sites, with many of their features. A Facebook user should feel at home there.

We ask ourselves whether - and how! – the emerging pedagogical principles can be used to promote widespread sustainable behaviour change through the web. A first, key question is: how might the principles for empowering design be adapted for use in designing and implementing a truly empowering web site?

We are in the process of compiling tentative responses. All input will be very welcome!

5. DIFFERENT ARENAS, DIFFERENT EXAMPLES

In this chapter we present different educational situations, with examples, and a discussion about how we have understood, used and modified the general principles. We also highlight emerging questions and concerns.

Informal adult education

Marilyn:

Our first challenge to ourselves even before we started Global Action Plan was: Can we find ways to make our own lifestyles more sustainable? And if so… will it necessarily entail a drop in our quality of life?

The answers were unequivocal. We could, and it didn't. Rather the contrary, we felt our quality of life was being enhanced in the process. This is a crucial point for anyone working with sustainable development. It's about lifestyle change, not lifestyle depreciation.

There are many people who disbelieve this. They say that sustainable development is, for the richer part of the world's population, a question of sacrifice: of giving up things we really want, and even believe we need, for the benefit of poorer people and future generations. Of course that's one way to approach it. But by working systematically with empowerment and consciousness-raising, we can learn to distinguish our true needs from our 'wants', and another world becomes not only possible but visible and enjoyable. (ref Kaushik)

There is a danger that the process of sustainable development is moving too slowly - some would say it's moving backwards, that we are backing into an increasingly unsustainable future. Perhaps in time the remaining available resources, human and other, will have dwindled to a level where only harsh sacrifice will do. And maybe not even that.

Is it perhaps already too late? No-one knows. And since no-one (literally no-one) can answer that question, each of us needs to decide: will I live my life as though there is still time, or will I live my live as though it's already too late?

It was easy for us to answer that question. If everyone lives as though it's already too late, then mostly probably it is (or soon will be). But if we all live as though there is a sustainable and rewarding future for humankind, then we have a sporting chance.

So our next challenge was: can we help other people to embark on or make progress with their own journeys to explore more sustainable lifestyles?

One point was clear to us from our own experience: moralizing and 'musts' don't work. Conventional pedagogy is based on the idea that the teacher knows the right way to do things, and will either tell the students, or - in the best case - help them to find out. We needed a different approach, where everyone teaches and everyone learns: what is coming to be known as a 'peer-to-peer' approach.

Another point was also clear, and it seemed at first to be in contradiction to the first point: people want clear instructions. By 1989, when we started, the world was already full of books about '1000 ways to save the world', and even databases of 'best practice'. The most common questions we received, then as now, were: 'Will it really make a difference?', and 'Where do I start?'.

Our response to this apparent paradox was to build our program around the core principle of inviting people to experiment.

This means that our materials offer carefully selected invitations to action. They are selected according to certain principles, and documented in the form of a cookbook with clear, simple instructions. In fact a cookbook is a good model for this type of curriculum design: the cook is totally in charge of the process, and receives highly structured help with implementation.

CASE: HOUSEHOLD ECOTEAMS, NETHERLANDS

PETER VAN LUTTERVELT

HTTP://WWW.VANLUTTERVELT.NL/

The Netherlands was, together with the USA, the first country to introduce a household EcoTeam program. The program drew inspiration from previous Dutch campaigns to empower people to reduce their use of gas for heating and cooking.

In many ways the Dutch EcoTeam program is still the most sophisticated of all; its counterparts in many other countries have also been successful in leading to long-term behaviour change, but none has been as successful in meticulously documenting the process. So the best available statistics are to be found in the Netherlands, where at least two universities have made use of them to conduct unique research into the behaviour change model and its effects.

SOME MILESTONES

After two years we had proved that the formula was working: we were achieving behaviour change with measurable results.

Then we started negotiating with other national NGOs so that they could deliver it to their members. This was not easy since there is a strong tendency for NGOs to view each other as competitors rather than colleagues. But the main women's organizations in the Netherlands took up the program. They loved the combination of empowerment and hard data. A lot of women were trained to multiply the program and started new EcoTeams.

Later, municipalities in the Netherlands started local Agenda 21 projects and because we were working locally we got support from them. After that the water and energy utilities started to sponsor the local offices – at that time, utilities were mostly still local rather than national.

Now, 2011, Global Action Plan Netherlands has been able to hand over the household and local community projects completely to partners, and is focusing on professional and workplace programs.

Harland et al (1997, 2006)

The regular education system

Olena:

The history of the Ukrainian educational Ecodemia project (from the combination of the words "ecology" and "democracy"), implemented 2005–09, is an example of successful cooperation between a national NGO, Teachers for Democracy and Partnership (TDP), and an international NGO, Global Action Plan International, with consultative status to the United Nations.

The project was aimed at secondary schools. Its purpose was to familiarize the teachers and general public of Ukraine with the experience and methodology of ESD, and to create appropriate teaching materials for students and teachers.

The Ecodemia project was launched in April 2005 when five schools in one city started testing ideas and materials offered by the international partners. For the Ukrainian teachers, researchers and educators it was a first introduction to Western educational experience for sustainable development. Then the teachers were offered recommendations for four lessons based on the idea of an empowering pedagogy, adapted by a team of teachers from TDP.

The next stage of the project was testing a specially developed educational game TellUs in Ukrainian schools for 5-6th grade pupils. The expert group of TDP and GAP prepared educational materials to help teachers and students; the educators requested qualitative and quantitative measurements regarding the use of family resources from students (water, energy, domestic garbage), and offered experience and skills to change lifestyles towards sustainable development.

Finally, in 2007–08, based on the results of the previous work, the international team developed a program for children called Lessons for Sustainable Development, unique in its objectives, content and methods of cognitive activity, which united all the previously developed and new materials and ideas; and started spreading it among Ukrainian schools. Monitoring has shown, among other results, that during these lessons the pupils changed their attitude and the attitude of their families to water and energy consumption. In almost all schools the project participants were able to involve other teachers, pupils and their parents in the program.

The final version of Lessons for Sustainable Development was approved in 2007 by the Ministry of Education, Science, Youth & Sports as an elective course for 8th grade pupils. By the end of 2008 about 100 schools in Ukraine had added the course to their syllabus.

In 2008–09, the continuation of the project was focused on the dissemination of innovative practices in Ukraine and general information for the teachers, parents and pupils. For this purpose, a special newsletter called Inspire to Act was founded for those interested in ESD in Ukraine.

In 2010–11 efforts were concentrated on developing ESD as a system for teaching children throughout secondary school, grades 3–9: see below, Case: ESD in Action.

INTEGRATED OR SEPARATE?

There is an on-going debate about whether ESD should be integrated into other school subjects, or should be a subject of its own. In summary, there is no doubt in our minds that we need both - at least for the foreseeable future.

The arguments for integration are well articulated. In most countries and at most levels of schooling, there is 'no room' in the curriculum for yet another subject; and anyway aspects of sustainability are needed and can be introduced into many subjects - some say all subjects. In fact, in this model 'all' teachers should be engaged.

This is all true, particularly if we focus on education about sustainability more than on education for sustainable development. And again, both are needed.

However, there are also some strong arguments for separation.
- *Education for SD is essentially trans-disciplinary. One of the sources of the accelerating unsustainability of our societies is the culture of analytical over-zealousness, leading to lack of overview and contextual understanding, and undervaluing the importance of synthesis.*
- *Education for SD is necessarily based on acquisition of life skills. Classes in maths, biology, geography, foreign languages… are not necessarily the best or even a reasonable place to do this.*
- *Not all teachers are capable of or indeed interested in teaching for SD. In fact, within current school and pedagogical systems it can be challenging enough to find a handful of teachers per school with this capability.*

Our tentative conclusions concerning a good model would be that
- *All teachers should be offered curricular material about SD to use in the course of their regular teaching.*
- *Lessons for SD should be offered as a separate subject; it could be as course material for an existing curricular topic, like civic studies - either for a whole year, or one term at a time.*
- *Lessons for SD can usefully be introduced at any school level.*
- *Teachers of lessons for SD should be offered in-service training, to enable them not only to master the content but also to acquire a deep understanding of the pedagogical needs.*

And about the lack of space in the curriculum: new subjects are introduced from time to time, and old ones disappear or are merged - often in response to developments in the labour market; and indeed it's important to equip our children with the knowledge and skills they will need to make a living. On the other hand, what could possibly be more important than equipping our children with the tools they will need to ensure a future for human civilization?

CASE: ESD IN ACTION, UKRAINE

Professor Olena Pometun

HTTP://ESD.ORG.UA/

This Ukrainian project, with support from Sweden, began with a one-year curriculum of 'Lessons for Sustainable Development' for use in Grade 8 of the Ukrainian school system. The structure is similar to that of the Dutch household EcoTeam program: pupils work in teams, with the teacher as coach, to make conscious choices to adopt more sustainable lifestyles.

The Grade 8 curriculum is very successful, is delivered by several thousand teachers in three regions of the country, and has been approved as an elective subject by the Ministry of Education.

The next step has been to extend the program to a full seven years: one lesson a week for sustainable development from grades 3 to 9; and to extend the program to other regions of the Ukraine. For this purpose, optional courses for grades 3, 4 and 9 have been developed, as well as extracurricular activities for the pupils of grades 5–7. From the 2011–12 school year, all these materials may be used in any Ukrainian school. Trainers at several regional centres for in-service training are qualifying to give the necessary teacher training.

CASE: NATIONAL STUDY OF UK SCHOOLS

A report from Ofsted, the British Office for Standards in Education, summarizes:

The schools that had made the greatest progress showed many of the following characteristics:

- *The plans for each year group included themes related to sustainability.*
- *Schemes of work and lesson plans emphasised enquiry and research, and provided opportunities for pupils to put these approaches into practice.*
- *Green issues, such as energy saving, recycling and healthy eating, were included in many aspects of the curriculum.*
- *Pupils were given opportunities to develop their speaking, listening and writing skills through work on sustainability.*
- *The schools periodically held themed weeks and high-profile events to promote an understanding of environmental and sustainability issues among pupils and parents. Examples included a yearly 'Energy Week' when every class focused on how to save water and to recycle more efficiently.*
- *Good use of the outdoor environment provided pupils with opportunities to learn in a practical context.*
- *Displays and artwork around the school highlighted the increased focus on education for sustainability and celebrated pupils' achievements in this area.*

The report also highlights the importance of strong support from the school principals to 'mainstream' sustainability into the curriculum:

"At the outset [of the longitudinal study], [few] of the schools included sustainability in their whole-school development plans. Those that improved most rapidly used the school development plan to give a high priority to sustainability and to link it to other aims."

CASE: THE MISSION, SWEDEN

Wolfgang Brunner, Solbergaskolan, Visby, Sweden

WORKING WITH "THE MISSION"

Students in grade 9 work with The Mission as a 'graduation assignment'. They are challenged to bring together their knowledge from different school subjects. The task begins when the pupils face the following mission:

You have been appointed by the Planetarian Council to plan and partake in the greatest adventure in the history of mankind: You shall equip a giant spaceship to make a journey of a range previously unheard of. These are the conditions:

- *The journey will last 6000 years*
- *You don't have to think about the ship's propulsion or the external hull.*
- *You have access to solar energy during the whole journey.*
- *No more than 100 persons are allowed aboard the ship at the same time.*

WHAT WILL YOU BRING?

If you give the students an open assignment of this kind you lead them into a process wherein they with their accumulated knowledge, experience, values and goals of life slowly explore both their inner self and the world outside. The energy or the motive power for their work comes mostly from the fact that they themselves are allowed to deal with the task in their own manner and decide which solutions they want to use.

The students want to have a rich and good life, so they search energetically for answers to all the questions that appear, because they want to know. They discover that they already have many of the answers, and they slowly put them together - and as with all creative work, they rejoice in their insights and are astounded at everything they have inside themselves.

We find that the students' discussions often follow a quite similar pattern. They form a kind of expanding spiral, time and again returning to the same questions but with increasing depth and width. (See chart below.)

The task forces the students to create a functioning whole built up of knowledge from many different fields. These fields of knowledge could be described in the following way:

- *How nature works (understanding basic principles of ecology)*
- *How society works (organizing a community that everyone benefits from)*
- *The meaning of life (looking for the deeper existential satisfactions)*
- *Sustainability (adding the "fourth dimension" that makes all this work together in a flourishing and sustainable way)*

WHAT I´VE LEARNED FROM "THE MISSION"

I have worked with "The Mission" since 1983. It has influenced my teaching and methods in many ways:
First I noticed everything the students didn´t know or had difficulties in understanding or discussing. How they struggled putting knowledge together from different subjects and how badly these often fitted. Our school system and curriculum really wasn´t designed for teaching about sustainability!

It has challenged me as a teacher and helped me to organize my teaching and prioritise what to put my efforts into. In that way "The Mission" also has become an evaluation of my own teaching abilities. - "I will try to do it better with the next group of students!" - became my pedagogic mantra!

It has helped me to new approaches, angles and evaluation methods. I have written textbooks and pedagogic manuals for teachers and developed many new practical and simple experiments for students

I also have used "The Mission" in teacher training, seminars and workshops addressing a broad variety of participants – teachers, teacher trainers, private companies, scientists and politicians. I have been invited to present my pedagogic ideas in all the Nordic countries and lately also in Japan and the USA.

CASE: MILLENIUM ESD, INDIA

CONTACT: SHANKAR MUSAFIR, RUMI EDUCATION PRIVATE LIMITED, DEHLI
MESD is a program in New Delhi, India, that offers pupils experiences to question and explore. The experiences are intended to help them define sustainability in their own way.

The first aspect of exploration is waste. Without giving any solutions, the students first conduct a waste audit of the school to understand the type, quality and quantity of waste. Next they sort the waste into different fractions. Then they explore local informal waste disposal and recycling activities. Kabadiwalas – local collectors of waste who collect different fractions (newspapers, bottles, metals etc.) – are interviewed. They are followed to their dump and the dump handlers are interviewed about the recycling channels for these different kinds of waste. The kabadiwala, who has very low social status, is invited as a chief guest to a school eco-club event.

Such projects give a holistic view of ESD – they are environmental projects because students explore and appraise the recycling industry. It's a social project because a kabadiwala who belongs to a totally ignored class is acknowledged; and because pupils learn interviewing skills. The economic aspect is obvious as kabadiwalas depend on waste for their livelihood. More such programs are planned on issues like traditional medicine.

The program is intended for basic schools grade 1 to 10, with a target group of 150 schools and around 37,500 students. During the pilot year (up to January 2010) six schools and around 150 students were involved. Two film snippets are available on YouTube: Koffee with kabadiwala and Waste Audit movie.

STRONG POINTS

- *We thought the students would react negatively to getting their hands dirty – sifting waste. But it was amazing to see that most of the students were more than enthusiastic to deal with waste and also in interviewing people.*
- *The learning value is not easily measured but every student had his or her own take away from the project.*

WISH-LIST/WOULD LIKE TO CHANGE OR INFLUENCE

- *Principals and teachers are so oriented towards projects that involve talking and presenting that they are a bit taken aback with things like interviewing people and getting hands on. Though every pedagogue talks about experiential learning, in practice it is rare.*
- *Principals and teachers often see their role as being to introduce advanced technology and science rather than (also) appreciating what is valuable in traditional systems.*

REFLECTIONS

- *Projects that go beyond 'spreading awareness' and 'preaching' to offer avenues of exploration have great learning value.*
- *Projects that appraise traditional systems have great value for ESD.*
- *ESD programs need not necessarily give solutions – they could just be explorations.*

Extra-curricular work in schools

CASE: SCHOOL ECOTEAMS IN POLAND

Zdzislaw Stan Nitak

HTTP://WWW.GAPPOLSKA.ORG/

GAP Polska's school program has been in operation since 1997. It follows the same basic structure as the household EcoTeam program.

This is a cooperative program between public schooling and civil society. The materials are developed and published by a national NGO, GAP Polska, which also delivers teacher training. However the actual teacher training usually takes place at a Teacher Training College, and entitles participating teachers to educational credits in the same way as other program delivered through the colleges.

Many books and other publications are now available. The basics are: "School Coach Manual for Sustainable Lifestyle" and "EcoTeam Coach Manual in Primary Education". Some materials are published and distributed to pupils: posters, CDs, brochures, and most is available on the GAP Polska website.

Every year about 200 new teachers take the program. Currently about 1000 teachers are actively delivering the program in their schools. An estimated total of 100,000 pupils have participated, and most of them have also successfully involved their families in the lifestyle work.

Monitoring of individual lifestyles is supported by a footprint calculator available on-line, and program participants report their results back to GAP. The current program is linked to the process of becoming a sustainable school with the possibility of awarding a school with the Green Flag (international) or Local Centre of Sustainable Activities (national) certificates.

CASE: YOUTH ECOTEAMS IN BELARUS

Irina Semko, National ESD Centre, Sakharov Environmental University, Minsk

This youth project was initiated by TreeVelop and IVN, two Dutch organizations, with the ambition of building on the successful Dutch experience with adult EcoTeams to
- Promote sustainable lifestyles
- Increase the awareness of the Belarusian population, and especially its youth, about the challenges and opportunities of sustainable development

- *Develop and deliver a practical program for sustainable development*
- *Support mini-projects that may serve as inspiration for others, so-called 'crystals of sustainability'*

There were three concrete objectives linked to these aims:
1. An increased sense of personal responsibility for environmental protection and sustainable development among Belarusian youth and their families, and behavioural change (more sustainable lifestyles)

2. Practical results and concrete examples of sustainable lifestyles reached by Belarusian youth, coaches and families

3. Strengthened capacity of the environmental civil society, increased availability of environmental education tools and lively twinning with international partners

The project reached a successful conclusion in 2011, including publishing workbooks for pupils and their teachers/ coaches, as well as a booklet about the 17 'crystals of sustainability' projects implemented by the youth teams.

CASE: DRAWING FOR LIFE

Comics in education – not a new concept. The communication power of simple drawings has been known since the Stone Age; and at least since the mid 20th century comic books have been used in both formal and informal education.

The additional power of the 'Drawing for Life' project, which began in Belarus and is gradually spreading, lies in the action component: the students are not readers but creators, learning to make their own comics and tell their own stories about sustainable development and sustainable lifestyle.

This methodology (ref Mehlmann et al) is evolving to contain three strands:
- *Storytelling with the power of myth: the common elements of a hero's journey*
- *How to tell a story through a series of drawings, in particular with few or no words*
- *The challenge of sustainable development, viewed from the perspective of a space visitor from a sustainable planet*

The project was pioneered in Belarus by Lydia Pshenytsyna with the support of the national centre of education for sustainable development, as well as of Global Action Plan International and the Swedish Institute. Lydia writes:

In the current global situation there is a need for global changes in culture and art, to enable young people to understand why and how they can adopt a responsible lifestyle. Comics are an excellent medium. The integrity of their heroes sets an ethical example. Comics push readers to develop their own lifestyle and live it later.

International trainer Esbjörn Jorsäter, Sweden, teaches teachers and youth leaders how to work with comics with children and youth, and is the author of a book on 'The hero's journey' in Swedish (2013). Esbjörn writes:

Comics can tap into deep strata of understanding with an archetypal cultural hero in focus. The hero's significance is measured by her or his deeds.

Participants do not need to be 'artists' or 'artistic' in any conventional sense. The power is in the story. Events since the Belarusian experiment include pupils in India and Pakistan preparing for and documenting a meeting across their conflicted boundaries; and youth in Kosovo, Albania and Macedonia meeting to draw their journeys towards sustainability.

CASE: ESD WITH PRE-SCHOOL CHILDREN

CONTACT: INGRID ENGDAHL

HTTP://WWW.OMEP.ORG.SE

OMEP, the World Organization for Early Childhood Education, reports on recent research demonstrating the competence of young children's participation and their ability to actively contribute to conditions and debates that affect them. Child participation is emerging as a marker of high quality practice in early childhood education. The UN Convention on the Rights of the Child lends global legislative weight to children's participation, as a human right and the capability of young children to actively engage in matters that relate directly to them

Participation is not only about interviewing children and listening to what they say; it is rather about actively involving children. This includes the awareness among teachers of the importance of capturing the children's interests and experiences so as to be able to take advantage of these in practice. Participation is also a prerequisite for action competence, one important embedded goal in education for sustainable development.

An OMEP study in Sweden in 2007–09, reported by Ingrid Engdahl, involved 533 children aged 1-6 years and 133 teachers and child care attendants plus around 20 OMEP members, teachers, psychologists, architects and researchers.

Results showed a major challenge to be the lack of traditions of taking children's ideas into account. In many ways adults think they know what's best for the children; they devise rules and routines that have a tendency to remain in force for long periods of time and even to outlast the children.

"ESD challenges the teachers' view of children. Its success is directly dependent on promoting an attitude depending on child participation and children's agency."

A final quote from a 5 year old child in Ireland to show how a child has grasped the whole idea of sustainable development – and in one sentence: *I think it might mean, like, to save the world for later.*

Workplace behaviour

ENGAGING EMPLOYEES

Many businesses as well as public agencies and NGOs have ambitions and programs that go beyond 'business as usual'. They may start with some kind of certification, for example ISO 14001 or 26001, or EMAS; or with involvement in a movement or program such as Global Compact/Global Reporting Initiative, Social Venture Network, or other groups working for social responsibility, carbon or climate neutrality, sustainable development…

The initial focus is often on technical or administrative investments and innovations. But sooner or later - assuming that the sustainability ambitions are genuine - it becomes apparent that the full potential of such investments can only be reached when the hearts, minds and hands of employees are engaged in adopting new behaviours and, finally, also in innovation: in the design of more sustainable ways to work.

LEADERSHIP AND PEDAGOGY

A critical point is leadership. If senior management is behind the initiative, there is every chance that results will be not only good, but surprisingly good, often surpassing ambitions. The role of the leaders is not to tell people what to do, but to inspire with a vision; and then to adjust management systems to reward progress in the direction of the vision. These points reverberate through the most successful case studies.

Additionally, there is a need for an adequate pedagogy: methods and tools to convey the vision and engage the creativity of employees in the search for ways to move towards the vision. In this, a workplace is no different from any other educational arena.

> 66 *If you want to build a ship, don't herd people together to collect wood and don't assign them tasks and work; but, rather, teach them to long for the endless immensity of the sea.*" — ANTOINE DE SAINT-EXUPERY

There are of course also cases of 'greenwash': workplace leaders whose wish for behaviour change is driven not by a longing for the immensity of sustainability, but rather by a desire to call their organization or product 'green' or 'socially responsible'. This can be regarded as an educational problem to the extent that they succeed in convincing their stakeholders that they are following a sustainable path. It under-scores the need for both serious accreditation or certification procedures, and for public education to enable stakeholders more easily to see through false claims.

ENTREPRENEURSHIP

Can education help new and existing entrepreneurs to meet 'triple bottom line' criteria? This means they should learn how to account for and achieve a return on investment not only in the financial sphere but also in the social and environmental dimensions of their operations.

An example is to be found in the Netherlands where MVO Nederland was founded for this purpose in the late 1990s with support from the Ministry of Economic Affairs. They jointly with Chambers of Commerce give presentations and master classes for SMEs (small and medium-sized enterprises); every Chamber of Commerce in the Netherlands has a CSR officer – some of them very active.

Another example is provided by the international ThinkCamp "Innovators for Sustainability" (see Case ThinkCamp), and its predecessor national programs in Germany and Austria.

CASE: INTERFACE: "TOWARD A MORE SUSTAINABLE WAY OF BUSINESS"

The USA-based international flooring company Interface embarked in 1994 on a daring journey to become sustainable. It consistently ranks top in independent sus-tainability surveys. Its program has included huge learning for thousands of employ-ees. One of their most basic conclusions is the vital role of a clear vision and mission - even if, like them, you have at the beginning little idea HOW you will fulfil your sustainability mission. The text below is from their web site.

Business and industrialism developed in a different world from the one we live in today: fewer people, less material wellbeing, plentiful natural resources. What emerged was a system that assumed infinite resources with little to no thought given to its impact. Today, that system no longer enhances our prosperity; instead, it is endangering it. When Interface saw itself as part of this system and the collective problem, we began a journey in a different direction, toward sustainability.

The Interface journey toward sustainability has been a momentous shift in the way we operate our business and see the world. We believe our journey can be a model for business in the next industrial revolution.

Our journey has been incredibly good for the business of Interface. As our founder and Chairman, and the leader of the Interface journey toward sustainability, Ray Anderson, has said:

> **"Costs are down, not up, dispelling a myth and exposing the false choice between the economy and the environment; products are the best they have ever been, because sustainability has provided an unexpected wellspring of innovation; people are galvanized around a shared higher purpose; the goodwill in the marketplace generated by our focus on sustainability far exceeds that which any amount of advertising or marketing expenditure could have generated."**

Interface's dedication to sustainability has evolved into the company's Mission Zero commitment — our promise to eliminate any negative impact Interface has on the environment by 2020. We hope our commitment will inspire you to create your own Mission Zero journey to sustainability.

The extraordinary story of Interface is also the story of an extraordinary individual, Ray Anderson. When he died in 2011, tributes flowed in from the whole world. Paul Hawken's contribution (ref) eloquently describes the impact of one person with a vision.

CASE: A VIETNAMESE EXPERIMENT

Contact: Giang Dang, Action for the City, Hanoi
Since the late 1990s several organizations in the Global Action Plan network have been developing and delivering so-called 'employee engagement programs' in Europe. The point of the programs is for employees to learn more about the vision of their management as regards sustainable development, and to contribute actively to moving towards the vision.

In 2008 a member in Vietnam, Action for the City (AfC), requested support to adapt and test the program on a small scale in Hanoi. The 'guinea-pig' clients were three NGOs - one of them AfC - that in principle were too small for this kind of program, but where management wished to pioneer and evaluate the method.

Results far surpassed expectations. Despite the small numbers of employees, their changed daily habits saved enough money to pay for the program and to fund a continuation and expansion.

EXPERIENCE OF THE EMPLOYEE ENGAGEMENT PROGRAM: RESPONSES TO FINAL QUESTIONS

What do we like most about the program, in retrospect?
- *We really acquired new habits, and we've retained them.*
- *It's empowering and democratic; stimulates initiatives from the staff*
- *The feel-good factor; proud to tell others, and can say we've done it ourselves*

- *We saved a lot of money - much more than we expected*
- *Team spirit; fun ways to relate to each other and pep each other*
- *The focused campaigns were effective*
- *We moved to a more sustainable office location…*

What could we do better/more of, now?
- *More topics, more actions - we have lists*
- *Analyse the data more thoroughly, to understand where the main benefits are coming from and how they might be enhanced*
- *Transport is a tough nut to crack, even though we made good progress*
- *Involve (even) more staff, bring new staff members on board*
- *Research better sources for purchasing*
- *Make the habits easier to keep - improve the convenience factor*
- *Overall, lifestyle is still 'westernizing' - how to counteract?*
- *Help/encourage the staff to take their new habits home*
- *Translate some of what we've learnt into guidelines and policies*
- *Cooperate with each other to produce better analyses, reports, research*
- *Find a good balance between empowerment and directives*
- *Scale up, reach out to others*
- *Move closer to a definition of what we mean by increasing sustainability ("Green Office")*

ACTION POINTS
1. Go further in own workplace
1.1 Re-energize the campaign, 1–2 topics per year
1.2 Offer an action team program to staff with a coach from AfC
1.3 Admin guideline AfC, input from others
2. Joint actions between all three organizations
2.1 Bulk paper ordering (also invite others)
2.2 New joint staff position (part- or full-time)
    - Documentation: collect/analyze results, write up
    - Research admin/technical solutions, eg paper suppliers
    - Coordinate actions
    - Develop guidelines
    - Research regarding offset
    - Outreach, ambassador
2.3 Regular coordination meetings
3. Reach out to others
3.1 Organize joint meeting to reach out to NGOs
3.2 Each will share information within own networks
4. Advocacy/social initiatives
4.1 Electric bike campaign
4.2 Green transport campaign

CASE: SCANDIC HOTELS: "GOOD TODAY, BETTER TOMORROW"

CONTACT: INGER MATTSSON, SCANDIC HOTELS
HTTP://WWW.SCANDICHOTELS.COM

The Scandic hotel chain began developing its sustainability program in 1993. It developed its own mix of leadership vision, expert advice, and employee education and engagement. Gradually the program extended from an initial focus on environment to encompass also social aspects of sustainability, with additional focus on accessibility for people with disabilities, and on health and safety issues.

As their slogan shows, they view their own sustainable development as a continuously on-going process. The text below is from their web site.

Now we see good environmental, economic and social considerations feature in our everyday decisions. Today, sustainability issues are high on the agenda for many companies. Scandic is proof that you can be progressive in these areas and achieve even better profitability along the way.

Our belief in the future is based on equal parts of sustainable proactivity as well as care and consideration for others. These are fundamental values that everyone within Scandic works to. We know that it is possible to reduce fossil carbon dioxide emissions. We think that health is an obvious focus. And we realise that accessibility is a must. Come to us any day of the week and you'll find team members who enjoy doing something they believe in. You'll see how together, we are turning environmental and social issues into natural, everyday actions. You'll get a glimpse of a world where the society around us is an asset.

We want to find a balance between the physical, emotional and spiritual needs that everyone has. It's a holistic approach and, if you ask us, a great way of looking at life.

REFLECTIONS FROM INGER MATTSON

Sustainable Business Manager at Scandic

It began with big changes. Or rather, with a huge number of simultaneous small changes. In 1993 there was a financial downturn in the world, and Scandic needed to increase income and reduce expenses. A visionary management team saw that an environmental program could lead to both: reduced costs for energy, waste, chemicals and water; and more visits from increasingly concerned travellers.

Every employee was invited to come up with ideas, after a short course based on the 'Framework' of The Natural Step. At these dialogue meetings at the hotels, ideas were spawned both for their own hotel, and for the chain. Within six months, 1 500 activities were started. That's the key to success in this work: engaging everyone, because everyone had something to contribute.

But that was only the beginning. The big stuff is challenging and inspiring, but keeping things going year after year, with smaller progress and sometimes even a step back, takes a different kind of leadership. Some of the educational things we've done and do to keep the forward movement:

- *We created an e-learning program for all new employees; participation gives access to staff benefits.*
- *We integrated environment into all our concepts. For instance, training for cleaners includes use of chemicals, sorting waste, turning off lights – as habitual behaviour.*
- *We created a new reporting tool, to enable us to monitor progress. Since 1996 every hotel reports every month on their energy, water, waste and chemicals use.*
- *We keep up a living dialogue throughout the chain, partly through having one person responsible in each hotel who keeps sustainability on the agenda.*

We also made technical and administrative changes, for instance:
- *We modified the hotel buildings and equipment to make it easy to save resources.*
- *We choose our suppliers carefully, and we ask them to help us keep an eye on our performance – for instance, to point out 'wrong'-looking orders; and we make suggestions for their product and delivery development.*
- *We subscribe to two 'green' labelling systems, the Nordic Swan and the EU ecolabel. Criteria for the labels are continually updated, so we are obliged to improve.*
- *We ask our guests for their opinions. And produce leaflets about our sustainability work. And publish reports on our web site, not least concerning progress over time.*
- *We created a building standard to make sure our renovations are as 'sustainable' as possible.*

Finally, and importantly, the top management team gives unqualified support to the program. They have a 'Compass for sustainable business' that is used in decision-making.

Our hotel chain is expanding, and integrating new hotels into the work is also part of our challenge. With a newly-built hotel and newly-recruited staff, no problem – in fact, a dream situation. When we acquire an existing operation we need to establish mutual trust, for example using a 'buddy system' in which the new hotel is supported by an 'old' one. With both new and acquired hotels we use a similar process to our first, big change: engaging all employees in short courses and dialogue groups.

Are we satisfied? No! And probably that's another key to success, to see our work as an on-going journey, not a destination. On the other hand we need to celebrate the milestones we pass, and I don't think we're good enough at that yet in Scandic. It's easy to fall into a rut, to believe that progress will inevitably continue to be made. We need to celebrate, and to keep renewing our materials and raising the ambition level.

CASE: DUTCH SUPPORT FOR SMES

CONTACT: PETER VAN LUTTERVELT

WWW.VANLUTTERVELT.NL

Social Venture Network 'spin-off' engages entrepreneurs in the Netherlands
In 2002, SVN Netherlands and the Ministry of Economic Affairs supported the start of a company called MVO Nederland to promote social responsibility especially among SMEs. MVO linked up with local chambers of commerce to give presentations and master classes for SME on how to become more sustainable and socially responsible.

'One of the best things we do is called "BrainTrainTours"', writes Peter Van Luttervelt of the SVN. 'It is high level consultancy for free, from network colleagues, inspiring for everybody, and of great practical use.'

A BrainTrain is initiated when a member company formulates a dilemma it faces in its progress towards sustainability. Other members are invited to visit the company for an evening, when the dilemma is discussed in teams. At the end of the evening all teams present their solutions.

CASE: THINKCAMP: INNOVATORS FOR SUSTAINABILITY

CONTACT: JOHANNES PFISTER

HTTP://WWW.THINKCAMP.EU/WIKI/DISPLAY/THINKCAMP

The ThinkCamp Entrepreneur program is an intensive coaching and training program to support emerging leaders to implement sustainable change in the launch of new enterprises, or to create new sustainable products/processes for existing organizations. The idea is to bring about sustainability – financial, ecological and social. The ThinkCamp organization is planned as a cooperative social enterprise.

The main target groups are emerging leaders, young entrepreneurs and leaders. During 2009 we reached 36 people in prototype programs (summer camps, dialogues etc.) in Germany, Austria and Jordan. We aim to reach 1,000 participants conducting 100 projects by 2015.

STRUCTURE

During the year the participants meet approximately every month for a week for learning and experience sessions. Between the meetings they work individually on their projects, being supported by internet coaching.

The monthly meetings are conducted at different locations (mountains, cities, islands) and enriched by visiting interesting organizations and discuss examples of sustainable development.

PEDAGOGY AND METHODS

Learning by doing, prototyping, learning by teaching, knowledge maps, flexible modules on demand, dialogue. Not a fixed curriculum but flexible knowledge access utilizing partners and experts.

We have developed an effective project phase plan with best practice tools in order to support and speed up the problem solving process and breakthrough innovation development.

Multinational examples

The question of how to accelerate learning becomes particularly interesting in an international context. There are so many factors to take into account, for instance

- *Different physical and social circumstances affect the facts to be offered to students concerning sustainable development*
- *Different cultures affect most aspects of programs, from what may appropriately be mentioned or suggested, to the type of language used and the style of illustrations*
- *Different educational infrastructure enables or hinders different delivery mechanisms, including for example training of teachers and coaches*

Nonetheless there are multinational programs, and their number is growing. Here are some reflections, and a few examples.

ADAPTATION CONSIDERATIONS

How easily can a program be transferred from one language and culture to another?

Marilyn:
Our own early experience in Global Action Plan was disheartening. The first transfers were spontaneous: a group in a new country found our program, translated the materials - and, in general, failed to achieve the results. On the other hand, some programs - such as EcoSchools, or Green Flag, and also our own later - are very successfully transplanted.

Our first conclusion was that there is a need for support for the transfer. Even if the initiative is spontaneous, it needs to be supported by training and coaching.

The most important focus for the training, at least in the case of a program intended to bring about lifestyle changes, seems to be methodological: not just in mechanical terms, but in terms of the heart and spirit of the pedagogy. This is difficult to convey in text (though we are doing our best with this book!); the easiest way is by workshop.

The question of *content* is more tricky.

There is often a given content from the point of view of knowledge transfer. If, for instance, the main focus is on human rights, then the basic content is more or less given by international treaties and agreements. If the focus is on ecological sustainability, there are certain inescapable principles. If the focus is on resource use, then at least energy and garbage are bound to be included.

In the case of ESD, all these topics can be brought into focus; but beyond knowledge transfer comes the invitation to action. And while the principles are indeed global, the actions need to be local: either local to the culture as a whole, or even local to a specific place or group. So here comes another level of need for support: a process by which to identify and test invitations to action.

CASE: GREEN FLAG: ECO-SCHOOLS

HTTP://WWW.FEE-INTERNATIONAL.ORG/EN/MENU/PROGRAMMES/ECO-SCHOOLS

The biggest single example of a multinational ESD program may be Green Flag, or Eco-Schools: a program for schools and pre-schools that aims to raise students' awareness of sustainable environmental development issues. It is a system for environmental management in schools, based on an ISO14001/ EMAS approach.

Eco-Schools is one of the programs of the Foundation for Environmental Education and is implemented through FEE Member organizations (one per country). Currently [2011], the program is being implemented in 50 countries around the world, involving nearly 50,000 schools, nine million students, 700,000 teachers and thousands of local authorities.

Eco-Schools is designed to implement sustainable development education in schools by encouraging children and youth to take an active role in how their school can be run for the benefit of the environment.

The Eco-Schools Program employs a holistic, participatory approach, combining learning and action, thus providing an effective method for improving the environments of schools and producing actual awareness raising and behavioural change in young people, school staff, families, local authorities, and so on, having significant repercussions in the local communities.

CASE: LIFE-LINK

CONTACT: HANS LEVANDER, LIFE-LINK FRIENDSHIP-SCHOOLS, UPPSALA, SWEDEN

Life-Link is an international program based in Sweden engaging 600 schools in over 80 countries. The basic approach is to offer participating schools a choice of over 50 concrete actions or projects. It is in two parts:

1. PEACE/CARE ACTIONS (PROJECTS, LECTURES)

Youth, usually aged 12-19, together with teachers, and if possible also parents and community resource people, select one or more of the "2 hours" or part-day actions proposed in the Life-Link Manual. The themes are Care for Myself - Care for Others - Care for Nature and Let's Get Organised. Each performed action is reported to Life-Link. The principal format is to select a topic, find a local expert, and organize an information and discussion event.

The Life-Link Manual - available from the 'Resources' section of their web site - also contains sections on project management and fund-raising.

2. SCHOOL LINKING

Once a school and its actions are listed on the 'in practice' section of the web site, the school can look for other schools that have performed similar actions, and can contact them directly in order to exchange experience and find out whether there is any basis for cooperation.

Strong points
- *The Life-Link ethics discussing and promoting each individual's responsibility for him/herself, for others, for nature, makes the concept of sustainability more clear for teachers and educational institutes.*
- *The Life-Link program promotes small "2-hour actions" to be performed at schools, and also interactive with the nearby society. Such a strategy and "ownership" helps to make the schools more recognized within the community, not least engaging parents in the actions.*
- *Life-Link offers no money to participating schools, and does not ask for money. This prevents any corruption or other unwanted dependence. A decentralized process is created with schools as owners of their locally performed actions.*

Wish-list
- *Life-Link has no resources to promote teacher training programs.*
- *Students at schools have asked for a follow up Life-Link program at the level of*

college or university. Also primary schools are not involved in the program, though some primary schools use the Life-Link manual and actions by themselves.
- *The website could be much more interactive.*

Reflections
- *The Life-Link program is by its character "crosscurricular". This is positive and necessary within a crosscurricular ESD dimension. On the other hand it is a challenge for teachers, used to educate within more focused subjects, and for planning of schools' curriculum. Adding the Life-Link ESD oriented actions as "extracurricular" lessons could solve such a problem, but on the other hand also put these social sciences activities on a lower priority and status level compared to natural sciences.*
- *Assessment of ESD-lifestyle achievements is important, but also more difficult than subjects like mathematics or biology.*

CASE: ÁNANDA MÁRGA GURUKULA

CONTACTS: DADA SHAMBHUSHIVANANDA, INTERNATIONAL TEACHER TRAINING, BASED IN SWEDEN, DIDI ANANDARAMA, GLOBAL COORDINATOR BASED IN CAIRO, EGYPT

Many ESD programs have taken their starting point in ecology, or even 'nature education', and have gradually expanded to include a broader view of environmental sustainability, social aspects, and sometimes also economic sustainability.

Ánanda Márga comes from the opposite direction. The starting point is an ethical and social education placing emphasis on the development of mature, empowered individuals. From there, they broadened their programs to include economic sustainability, and are now including aspects of environmental sustainability.

The network of schools spans over fifty countries with over 1000 kindergartens, primary schools, secondary schools, colleges and children's homes that have been established over the past 30 years.

Paraphrased from their web site: The Gurukula system of education is the oldest on our planet, tracing its roots back 10,000 years to the time of ancient civilization and dedicated to the highest ideals of all-round human development: physical, mental and spiritual. All aspects of the individual are developed using an integrated curriculum that empowers the students' self-knowledge, and develops the confidence and empathy to use knowledge in service to society.

WHAT MAKES AN ÁNANDA MÁRGA SCHOOL SUCCESSFUL?

The school needs to have a very alive, vibrant school administration that thrives on great ideas and are enthusiastic to implement them. Those schools grow and grow in innovative material. From these schools we pool the innovative practical, class-room-tested ideas of sustainable teaching modules.

In many poorer countries our schools are service projects to very needy communities. It seems they need help on all levels, basic learning environment, educational and sustainable practices.

Naturally our best schools had a lot of interaction and exposure to educational practices, sustainable living etc. which is taken by the teachers and parents right into the classroom. These things are lacking in our school communities in India and Africa and many other places. Conclusively more interaction, communication, exchange between projects that are successful and those that need help is the way to go.

An interesting effect is that although we are focused primarily on our own network yet there is 'spillover' to the local community as teachers from neighboring schools come and attend our in-house teacher training programs. As our capacity grows we would like to wide our circles to reach more schools in this way.

CASE: THE NATURAL STEP

CONTACT: ÅSA STENBORG, DET NATURLIGA STEGET, STOCKHOLM, SWEDEN

The Natural Step (TNS) is a Swedish-based NGO, now with branches in several countries on all continents, rooted in a scientific consensus process to derive and test robust principles for ecological and social sustainability as well as strategic guidelines to approach compliance with those principles.

Since the start in 1989 it has been principally associated with its unifying framework for strategic sustainable development (FSSD). It contains five levels (i) a scientific description of the biosphere with its human societies, (ii) a principled definition of social and ecological sustainability in this system, (iii) strategic guidelines to approach compliance with the principles, (iv) concrete actions and (v) a toolbox for monitoring of (iv) actions to be (iii) strategic to arrive at (ii) sustainability in the (i) system. The FSSD is the focus of science, research, education and consulting programs, primarily for municipalities, business and universities, offered by the foundation, its branches, and associates. Increasingly, courses are offered via Internet. There is also an international university masters program 'Strategic Leadership towards Sustainability' based on the foundation's framework, run at Blekinge Institute of Technology in Sweden.

From the onset in Sweden in the 1990s, the approach of TNS was remarkably successful in bringing about concrete change in some Swedish business organizations and municipalities, the role models of which have now influenced thousands of organizations across the globe (business, municipalities and universities).

In 2008 the foundation strengthened its research base by co-founding 'Real Change': an international alliance of universities examining the science of sustainable development in collaboration with businesses, NGOs, communities and policy makers. FSSD serves as the shared mental model of the program.

Internet as a tool for learning

The power of the internet as a promoter of more-or-less unconscious behaviour change is probably unparalleled in history. Around the world, people - especially young people - are rapidly adopting lifestyles unfamiliar or even alien to an older generation; and city-dwellers are adopting lifestyles that may be almost incomprehensible to their village counterparts.

A pivotal question is whether the internet can also be a tool for promoting conscious lifestyle choices; and if so, how it can be conscripted to the service of sustainable development.

One approach is to create a specific behaviour-change vehicle linked to 'hot' topics. Since about 2006 there has for instance been a flurry of web sites inviting the general public, or some sector of it, to save energy. These have not been notably successful; nor have they been designed with the principles of an empowering pedagogy in mind, so possibly there is scope for improvement. Such sites will however always, almost by definition, have difficulties in attracting visitors other than those already engaged in the topic.

Is it at all possible to reach out to people who lack prior belief in their ability to make a difference - or even insight into the need?

The huge dissemination success of the social network sites needs closer examination. It seems that people all over the world are longing for opportunities to become accepted members of new, electronic communities. Can this longing also provide energy and input for an ESD program?

To date (2012) we know of only one national-scale experiment, in Norway, and it is not entirely useful as a role model for others, as described below. We do however believe we will be able to extract new knowledge from the Norwegian experience.

In addition, we offer the experience from the UK of a single-subject program for schools dealing with the topic of food and its environmental impact. Called 'Appetite for Action', this program is also non-typical but can surely teach us something about the potential.

CASE: NORWEGIAN "CLIMATE CLUB"

CONTACT: GRØNN HVERDAG, OSLO, NORWAY

The Norwegian online 'Climate Club' was started by a national NGO, Grønn Hverdag ('Green Living') late in 2008. It could be said to be a cross between GAP's household EcoTeam program, and sites like Weightwatchers and Facebook.

The Norwegian Ministry of Environment sees it as a national tool to be offered by public agencies to the general public – a factor that cannot necessarily be duplicated in other countries. Major business partners are also involved, including VG,

Norway's largest daily paper. Every Norwegian municipality is invited to add its own page with specifically local 'green' actions.

Initial uptake was disappointing, partly because of severe technical 'teething problems'. However by mid 2010 around 40,000 people had taken the 'How green are you?' test, and resource savings as a result of user actions were being aggregated and displayed on the site.

From the site: The Climate Club is a free tool for greener living. As a member, you can

- *Keep track of your CO2 emissions.*
- *Compare with friends, colleagues, etc.*
- *Receive tips about more things that you personally could do.*
- *Share your knowledge and experience with others.*
- *Take the test and find out how green you are!*

No-one can do everything, but everyone can do something. You are important – your actions count!

CASE OF A SINGLE-TOPIC PROGRAM: 'APPETITE FOR ACTION'

CONTACT: LUKE WYNNE, GLOBAL ACTION PLAN UK, LONDON

> 66 *"Appetite for Action helps children make the connection between the environment, the food they eat and the food they throw away."*

Appetite for Action is the name of a three-year online program launched in January 2009 by Global Action Plan UK. It addresses schools with a program focused on sustainable food.

The program was based on the concept of campaigns, with prizes for schools showing the best results. Schools could take on one of three challenges: Greener Grub, Get Growing, or Reduce Rubbish, plus use the online resources available to encourage children to waste less food, grow their own, and understand how composting works. Each participating school had its own profile page on the web site.

The first campaign, which lasted until June 2010, attracted 1,864 schools in the UK, and some in Ireland.

An unusual feature of this program is that it was developed in cooperation with, and funded by, a TV channel, Sky Channel. The school that was judged the overall campaign winner hosted a TV show.

6. EDUCATIONAL ASPECTS OF SUSTAINABILITY AND DEVELOPMENT

With a focus on education for (rather than about) sustainable development, the teacher should not need to be an expert on sustainability. On the contrary, the teacher who successfully teaches this subject is likely to be a generalist rather than a specialist (see section Teacher's competencies).

Nonetheless, educators may find it helpful to have some knowledge of sustainable development as a background to helping students do their own research. In particular in this chapter we would like to

- *Paint a picture of the transdisciplinary nature of SD*
- *Illuminate some important aspects of SD that are often overlooked*
- *Expose some of the myths that tend to cloud our thinking about ESD: the beliefs and habitual thoughts that have brought us into the present perilous position need to be re-examined*
- *Focus on some of the key questions that are currently (2012) being discussed in relation to sustainable development*

This chapter gives a very brief overview, as background material for teachers and others. It is not intended to be complete. Our ambition is rather to raise some critical points that can help bring a transformative perspective to the wealth of information that is readily available in many media.

One way to raise critical points is to identify beliefs about sustainable development and society that are widely held despite being inaccurate. We call them 'misleading myths'.

MISLEADING MYTH NO. 1:

ESD is the same as environmental education or nature studies.

What does the United Nations say?

In 2005 the United Nations inaugurated a Decade for Education for Sustainable Development, coordinated by UNESCO. They identify a number of 'key action themes' for the decade:

- Gender equality
- Health promotion
- Environment
- Rural development

- Cultural diversity
- Peace and human security
- Sustainable urbanization
- Sustainable consumption

These themes cut across the more usual categorization of 'ecological, social, and economic sustainability' - but clearly social sustainability has a strong role. And equally clearly, ESD is cross-disciplinary, involving both teachers and students as whole persons:

> **66** *Sustainability is co-ordinated action on the physical, intellectual, ethical, emotional and spiritual levels to ensure the full expression of the human drive, at the individual and collective levels, to expand in harmony with the environment."* — MARCUS BUSSEY

Economic sustainability, as such, is conspicuously absent from the UNESCO list. Bernard Lietaer wrote in 2008: "We have now entered a period of unprecedented convergence of the four planetary issues - financial instability, climate change, unemployment and the financial consequences of an aging society."

Even more critical is the apparent absence of a cross-disciplinary dimension rooted in 'strong sustainability': the concept that sustainable development is not a question of adjusting existing systems, but of transforming them. Without this dimension the whole concept risks flying apart into ever-smaller fragments.

MISLEADING MYTH NO. 2:
....

ESD can be divided up among existing disciplines.

'Strong sustainability'

SWEDESD, the Swedish International Centre of Education for Sustainable Development, bases its work on a concept of 'strong sustainability':

One thing is not negotiable and cannot be questioned – the limitations set by the planetary boundaries.

Strong sustainability is about this very fact that all human activities must be conducted within the realm of the biosphere's limits, as the Earth's natural systems and resources are the fundamental base of all human existence and activities. The services provided by our ecosystems supply oxygen, fresh water and the possibilities to grow or collect food products as well as other life-sustaining functions. It is also the natural systems that, together with human input, provide the constituents for the resources we have available for economic activity.

Today we are not living off the interest from this capital, but are actually consuming resources faster than they have time to replenish. Natural capital must be maintained and enhanced, as the functions it performs cannot be duplicated by manufactured capital.

Strong sustainability may further be explained as environment and the natural resources being the overarching foundation for society; and economy, in turn, a subset of society.

We are already using up planetary resources at a rate far greater than they are being replenished - and the human population is still expanding. Clearly this cannot be dealt with by adjusting existing systems. Either we transform the systems, or radically reduce the population. See further Eric Neumayer on Strong Sustainability (ref).

MISLEADING MYTH NO. 3:

We can keep our current habits and institutions; with some adjustment, they will take us to a sustainable future.

❝ *"If we overdraw our ecological accounts, we are undermining our future."* — MICHAEL MEACHER, FORMER UK MINISTER OF ENVIRONMENT

❝ *"The world will no longer be divided by the ideologies of 'left' and 'right,' but by those who accept ecological limits and those who don't."* — WOLFGANG SACHS, HEAD OF THE PROJECT GLOBALIZATION AND SUSTAINABILITY, WUPPERTAL INSTITUTE (REF)

NATURAL CAPITAL

'Capital', in the sense of natural, human and social capital, is a word derived from its use in economics, where it stands for the basic wealth that shall, for healthy development, not be diminished. If your capital is safely invested, you can safely spend the interest - the money that is paid to you by other people who are making use of it. If you increase your capital, you also increase your wealth and income - and can maybe support a bigger family. This is the classical picture.

The analogy is reasonable. For billions of years the planet has been increasing its natural capital: its capacity to support increasing populations of increasingly diverse species. From a purely human point of view, natural capital is the capacity of the planet to keep US alive; which in turn depends on its capacity to maintain all the other millions of species, from bacteria to insects, on which our lives depend. (Hawken et al, 2010)

The bad news is that the planet's natural capital is now in steady decline, as a direct result of human intervention. See, for instance, the concept of overshoot, tracked by the Global Footprint Network (ref). A top priority for sustainable development must be to reverse this trend – or to be prepared to settle for a MUCH smaller family of humankind.

STRONG SUSTAINABLE DEVELOPMENT

Seen through this lens, sustainable development becomes a process of moving towards restoration of natural capital, to a level where humankind is once again living within the limitations set by planetary boundaries.

We may perhaps assume that beyond this desired culmination there will continue to be development, as both planetary boundaries and the needs and capacities of humankind shift. However, this definition is not enough if we are to talk about truly strong sustainable development.

The arguments in favour of strong sustainability are totally compelling: if we don't do it, we all die. The science is clear, and has been for at least 20 years – see for instance the work of The Natural Step; and long before that, of others such as Buckminster Fuller, whose prolific life of exploration, discovery, invention and teaching was driven by his intention "to make the world work for 100% of humanity, in the shortest possible time, through spontaneous cooperation without ecological offense or disadvantage of anyone."

 We must all live together as brothers, or we will all perish together as fools." — MARTIN LUTHER KING JR.

Still, for some reason, we are backing into an increasingly unsustainable future. Not only are we not achieving strong sustainable development; we are practicing and in some aspects actually accelerating unsustainable development.

So we need to ask ourselves: Why? How is this possible, when we have the temerity to call ourselves homo sapiens?

It seems clear that the drivers of this development are not to be found in the natural environment. They can be sought inside people, in the form of instincts, beliefs, values, and habits, and in communities of people – in the social, economic and developmental contexts.

SOCIAL SUSTAINABILITY

Socially sustainable development is both a necessity in itself, and a necessary step towards environmental sustainability.

Many of today's global problems are social: poverty, malnourishment, lack of access to health care and education, vandalism, terrorism, crime, drugs, trafficking, domestic violence, disenfranchisement, homelessness, hopelessness… the list could be made much longer.

These phenomena are not only unworthy of civilized societies (or planets) but also contributors to environmental destruction. Unless we can create more civilized societies, we will be unable to come to grips with the bleak fact that the resources necessary to maintain human life on earth are diminishing, at an accelerating pace. As noted above, we are using up our 'natural capital', faster each year.

MISLEADING MYTHS NOS. 4 & 5:

The State must legislate so that people behave more sustainably, even if they object. The State is helpless in the face of people's determination to over-consume.

TOWARDS UTOPIA?

Social sustainability is in the first place about societies that work, in the sense that they function satisfactorily for all people. This is the dream of many utopians. Why should we believe that we can create such a society now, when it seems all attempts so far have foundered?

Well, necessity is a tough teacher. And perhaps the convergence of rising populations with dwindling resources, creating a 'tipping point' beyond which human societies simply cannot be maintained, will prove a sufficient incentive. It might do, if only 'human nature' is not, as some people claim, irrevocably selfish, greedy, violent - in short, ineducable. Are we like that?

Fortunately, the most recent science seems to show that we are at least as strongly 'programmed' for other qualities with much higher survival value, like cooperation, empathy, fairness, and efficacy.

MISLEADING MYTH NO. 6:

People are naturally selfish, greedy, and violent. These characteristics will always dominate any human society.

So the key question is: what stops us from bringing these qualities to the fore? Frances Moore Lappé (2011) writes: "I believe the evidence shows that three conditions, in particular, lead humans to no good. They are concentration of power, anonymity, and scapegoating." All three have strong implications for education, and in particular for ESD.

To this list we would add a fourth item, which indeed can be a consequence of any or all of the first three: the experience of injustice and random unfairness in society.

SOCIAL AND HUMAN CAPITAL

Natural capital, and its analogy to economic capital, were mentioned in the section on Strong Sustainability. Other expressions that are increasingly used are 'human capital' and 'social capital'. Here, the analogy is less close.

Human capital is widely regarded as the knowledge and skills of individuals, in which cornerstone elements could be said to be critical thinking, self-knowledge, empowerment, and communication skills.

Cornerstone skills contributing to 'human capital': critical thinking, self-knowledge, empowerment, communication skills.

There is no sense, analogous to economics, in which this capital can be spent or used up, since it increases with use. It can be eroded by disempowering systems and lack of information, or direct misinformation or propaganda, but not erased or used up.

Nonetheless it can give a useful perspective on ESD: our work should increase the human capital in the service of sustainable development.

It could be argued that any major increase in human capital will serve the cause of sustainability, simply because people with these skills and this knowledge will tend to make more sustainable decisions. This argument is backed by both research into 'human nature', and by surveys in many countries showing that a majority of people long for a society that is, in fact, more sustainable.

True, these longings do not translate easily into everyday action. This can no doubt be partly attributed to hindering infrastructures, but has also been shown to be strongly linked to deficiencies in the cornerstone skills.

MISLEADING MYTH NO. 7:

'People' are more interested in ever-increasing consumption than in safeguarding our common assets.

For social capital, the analogy to wealth could be seen to be capacity: a collective capacity to safeguard the interests of the collective. Like economic wealth, it is 'neutral' in that it can be used equally for sustaining all life, or for sectarian or destructive activities such as waging war.

Often mentioned as basic components of social capital are solidarity and social cohesion. Both of these build upon the question of trust - which is of course also the basis of modern economic capital. In order for social capital to serve the cause of sustainable development, mutual trust needs to develop beyond the level of 'the clan'.

How mutual trust can be fostered is a research topic, not least in games theory. The basis is observed to be reciprocity or mirroring. Interestingly, the 'winner' is always the one who consistently behaves in a cooperative way, switching to competition only when (but immediately) another party does so, and immediately switching back when the other party does so. This, then, is also a skill that can be taught.

MISLEADING MYTH NO. 8:

The skills needed for social sustainability cannot be taught.

FOUR DIMENSIONS OF SOCIAL SUSTAINABILITY

If we turn around the 'hindering factors' identified above, we can postulate four key dimensions of social sustainability: empowerment, democracy and accountability, personal responsibility, and security.

- *Powerlessness and empowerment*
- *Democracy and accountability*
- *Personal responsibility*
- *Security*

POWERLESSNESS AND EMPOWERMENT

A feeling of powerlessness - inability to choose or exercise influence - accompanies unsustainable development. Certainly the problems can seem overwhelming, especially in the face of disempowering media, and what are frequently perceived as political impotence and corporate greed.

Nonetheless there IS scope for action, by every individual. And many individuals with a sense of personal empowerment - as opposed to formal power - can change a whole society. In the theory of social diffusion, as few as 12-15% can make the difference when the circumstances are right. In the experience of GAP, an even smaller proportion can be effective.

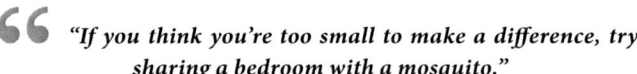 *"If you think you're too small to make a difference, try sharing a bedroom with a mosquito."*

So is it all personal? Can individuals succeed in creating or enhancing democracy, participation, justice, welfare, security? Is it the work of individuals to reach the UN goals of gender equality, health and wellbeing for all, cultural diversity, and peace and human security? No wonder if you feel yourself staggering under such a burden.

And yet… society is made of individuals. Without reaching out to individuals, wherever they may be in society, sustainable development remains tantalizingly out of reach. And on the other hand, if each one of us does the best we can, here and now, we will already have a far more sustainable society. When we talk to each other, listen to each other, join forces across social and other conventional barriers, we can accomplish almost anything. This is the premise upon which the World Social Forum (ref Whitaker) was created, and continues to grow.

"Scientists at Rensselaer Polytechnic Institute (ref) have found that when just 10 percent of the population holds an unshakeable belief, their belief will always be adopted by the majority of the society."

MISLEADING MYTH NO. 9:

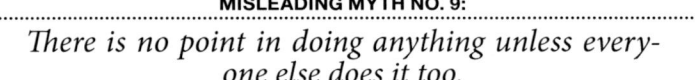

There is no point in doing anything unless everyone else does it too.

A pedagogy that enables and encourages individuals of all ages and from all sectors of society to reach out to each other, to engage in dialogue, and to support each other to establish more sustainable belief systems must surely be a cornerstone of sustainable development.

DEMOCRACY AND ACCOUNTABILITY

If anonymity is a major hindering factor, then sustainability needs also to build on democracy and accountability: accountability of both individuals and organizations for their actions, with full transparency for democratic insight and evaluation, and a judicious combination of representative and participative democracy.

To build such a society, there is a need for increasing skills and empowerment of individuals: empowerment to dare to support accountability, skills in critical thinking, the ability to evaluate and to make democratic decisions. Training and supporting these skills is an essential component of ESD at all levels. Here too, nurturing non-violent dialogue is an important tool.

In saying this, we are also saying that ESD, while non-sectarian, is not neutral. There are values that are basic to any community striving for sustainability.

PERSONAL RESPONSIBILITY

The antidote to 'scapegoating' is a culture of personal responsibility free from shame and blame. The potential for ESD to inculcate such a culture must be reckoned as one of its most powerful mechanisms.

This is particularly important in the light of our own collective ignorance about what sustainable societies might look like. On our journey, we will all inevitably find or decide that we have made mistakes. If sustainability is to have a chance, we need to squeeze every gram of learning out of those mistakes. Being ashamed, or blaming someone else, is a learned response in many cultures today, and it is a huge barrier to real learning.

MISLEADING MYTH NO. 10:

Some (other) people are responsible for the mess
we are in, and they must be shamed into changing
their ways.

Personal responsibility is also a factor in decision-making and negotiating skills. If the research from games theory is correct, we need to teach cooperation as the basic negotiating stance: the art of seeking out win-win solutions. And we need to teach rapid mirroring, so that a switch of behaviour by one party (from cooperation to competition or vice versa) is immediately mirrored by the other.

SECURITY

There is a sense in which 'feeling safe' is the basis for all sustainable development. A population that has its basic needs assured, including the need for fair treatment and recourse to the law, is far more likely to build a sustainable society than one where people are constantly worried about their basic conditions for survival, or feel unfairly treated or discriminated against.

Education that addresses social aspects of sustainable development is linked in terms of content with civics education curricula that already exist in many countries. The purpose of civics education in most modern democratic countries is to foster understanding and respect for the values of democracy, human rights, life and dignity, and the protection and personal responsibility of every individual; and the capacity and competence to act in accordance with these values.

MISLEADING MYTHS NOS. 11 & 12:

Experts must tell everyone what to do. There is no need to consult everyone – some groups have nothing to contribute.

It does not matter whether we consider education for SD as a part of civics education, or vice versa, it is much more important for this education not only to promote accumulation of civic knowledge and skills in students, but also to involve them in real action and form on-going behaviour patterns - conscious, responsible, and productive in relation to their own social life and the lives of others.

The current (2012) strong grass-roots movements demanding democracy, transparency and social justice in many countries eloquently illustrate the power of individuals translated into collective action. They give us a glimpse of the transformational potential. (ref Gelder)

TALKING AND LISTENING

A key element of social capital is often identified as 'cohesion', meaning the extent to which people are able and prepared to work together for their common good.

Cohesion in turn hinges upon trust; and trust is generated in social exchanges, including dialogue. Social sustainability is, importantly, about the quality and quantity of conversations we have about the kind of society we want – and don't want.

CONVERSATIONAL APPETIZERS

In a paper called 'Living Well on One Planet', Mathis Wackernagel (ref) makes the point that we need much more discourse on the subject of sustainable development:

"We have a conversation deficit – the physical limiting factor is the regenerative capacity of the earth, but a societal limiting factor is the appetite for sustainability; it is essential to get people 'hungry', to build the appetite for sustainability, and the permission to make the decisions to work towards it."

This is a challenge in a consumption-oriented society because it implies building a hunger for less rather than more. In a society in which personal identity is often linked to material possessions, it means establishing new status symbols, creating and exchanging new stories about who we are and what we value. We need to learn to 'boast' about the things we have chosen NOT to have; and to talk about our values, dreams, hopes for a liveable future.

THE QUALITY OF LISTENING

In most modern societies, the ability to talk is more highly rated than the ability to listen. We believe we listen, but in fact we are often paying more attention to our own inner dialogue

'Do I agree with this?'

'Do I like this person?'

'I wonder what s/he thinks of me...'

'I wonder whether it will rain'

'Did I remember to give my door key to the neighbour?'

'What can I possibly say in reply?'

'I must get that puncture fixed before I go home'

than to the words and intentions of the speaker.

Listening is a skill that can be (and is) taught. Examples are Active Listening (ref) and Deep Listening. It is a basic SD skill – basic to critical thinking, and indeed basic to self-knowledge and self-empowerment.

This essential work of conversation – of talking and listening to each other as a preliminary to, and as a part of, initiating change – can take place in any arena. There is no need to wait for a special forum. Just do it – at work, at school, in the clubhouse, in the bus queue or tenants' meeting.

CRITICAL THINKING

Education for sustainable development, as well as modern life in general, requires that the student does not simply acquire knowledge and tools to keep, for lifetime use. Rather, s/he needs to acquire the skill to create new, creative, transformatory tools.

This requires, among other things, the development of critical thinking, defined as the ability to thoughtfully relate to reality, to identify and objectively evaluate information received, to compare and analyse different points of view, to understand the complexities and contradictions of perceived phenomena. That is, it helps to find new ideas and meanings (ref Dewey). A person with well-developed critical thinking is better able to learn from experience and solve personal and social problems.

> 66 *"Critical thinking is the use of those cognitive skills and strategies that increase the probability of a desirable outcome... purposeful, reasoned and goal directed – the kind of thinking involved in solving problems, formulating inferences, calculating likelihoods, and making decisions..."* — D. HALPERN (1996)

When we think critically, not only do we assess the results of thought processes - how good our decisions were, or how well we coped with the task. Critical thinking also includes an assessment of the thinking process: the course of reasoning that led to our findings, or those factors that we have taken into account when making decisions.

In addition, people with well-developed critical thinking are characterized by the fact that they tend to:

- *Ask questions*
- *Base judgments on evidence*
- *Look for links between objects*
- *Be true to themselves*

- *Give the benefit of a doubt*
- *Be intellectually independent*
- *Be difficult to manipulate*

An uncritical perception of human reality is, on the other hand, evidence of intellectual and political immaturity, often leads to an inflated idea of personal merits and abilities, inhibits and blocks the process of personal and social growth.

The main objective of training critical thinking as a component of ESD is precisely in the development of the students' intellect, enabling them to learn and act independently. In this connection, activities focused on reflection are especially important.

CONFLICT AND DISAGREEMENT

Does this mean we should always agree about everything? Not at all!

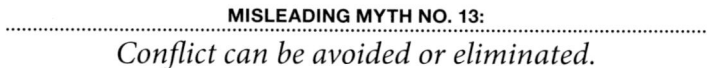 *"If two people agree about absolutely everything, one of them is not necessary."* — ITCHAK ADIZES

What is important is how we express our disagreement. From the bible (St Matthew) to Mao's Little Red Book we hear the same message: criticize the action (or opinion) but not the person. We are all different people, and inevitably this means that we view reality from different perspectives. There is a big difference in the quality of communication between *"You are wrong!"* and *"My experience has led me to a different conclusion."*

There are many schools of thought regarding the handling of conflicts and peace-building. A basic tenet of many of them is that conflict 'is' – neither good nor bad, but a fact of life. We need to learn to handle it rather believing it should not exist.

One approach that we have found useful in education is the concept of Non-Violent Communication (ref Rosenberg). Non-violent communication helps reduce tensions, and build more trustful relationships.

MISLEADING MYTH NO. 13:

Conflict can be avoided or eliminated.

DIVERSITY

'Biodiversity' is a word that has entered our vocabularies and consciousness over the past few decades. It is indeed a critical component of 'natural capital'. In the same way, cultural diversity is essential to the formation and maintenance of social capital. And cultural diversity, as noted above, can only flourish when rooted in trust.

WHEN WE TRUST - AND WHEN WE DON'T

There is an old saying that I trust you to the extent that I believe you resemble me. The bigger the perceived difference, the lower the level of trust. When two people talk, the quality of their exchange depends very much on their previous opinions of each other - even if they have never met before. Not least, assumptions of superiority and inferiority affect the words we use, the tone of voice, how we interpret the words of the other person.

In most societies today there are many cultural divides to bridge. In some cultures people of different age groups seldom meet, whereas in other countries it is part of the social fabric that at least three generations live together and interact on a daily basis. In other societies it may be that men and women, or different ethnic groups or religions, have different and separate cultures. Often, migrants are regarded with mistrust. These stereotypes are to be found in all cultures and ages; and since they distort our communications, they are an obstacle to both democracy and sustainable development.

Beginning to interact with people whom we have previously regarded as 'not one of us' carries its own challenges.

> 66 *In every encounter with a person from a different culture, we can choose to relate to the familiar or to the exotic. Or, we can turn our attention from both poles and choose to meet in the space between us. There, in the silent space between, a new, intercultural quality can emerge."* — MIRIAM SANNUM

Contemporary ethnic, cultural, confessional, linguistic and other diversity is the common heritage of all humankind. Once we learn to see past the stereotypes and establish trustful communication, this diversity can bring us innovation, creativity and cooperation – and joy.

MISLEADING MYTHS NOS. 14 & 15:

"I have no prejudices. I regard everyone as my equal." People can be commanded to 'respect' others.

We give an example from "Lessons for Sustainable Development" of a lesson in diversity.

STEREOTYPES AND DIVERSITY

The teacher invites students to do the following exercise.

Sometimes we imagine we know how someone will always act in a certain situation. For example, many other countries believe that all Ukrainians love bacon and all Italians love spaghetti, that the Germans are punctual, and Estonians slow. Such ideas are called stereotypes: generalized and simplified features that interfere in the reality of communication.

Here is an exercise to check your own any stereotypes; complete the following sentences:

- *Most of all I like people who ....*
- *Women are better able to ...*
- *Men are better able to ...*
- *All older people ...*
- *I love to communicate with my own age group, because ...*
- *I never trust people who ...*
- *I think a real Ukrainian ...*
- *People who do not speak my native language are ...*

Review what you wrote and try to determine where you have revealed stereotypical views. Discuss in your team why they arose and how they can interfere in your life. Compare your results. Do you have something in common? Pay more attention to such ideas. They are the most harmful, because common to many. Share your findings with other teams.

Next step: students consciously accept the description and plan how to be less prejudiced.

WHY ACT?

Stereotypes prevent us from communicating because they prevent us from seeing the other person as s/he really is: original, creative, not like others. Getting rid of stereotypes helps us to get acquainted with different people and enjoy the wonderful diversity of the world.

HOW TO ACT?

- *Observe your own behaviour and find patterns that prevent you making good contact with other people*

- *When talking to someone, remind yourself (and others) that people are different and have the right to be so*
- *Look for the good of all those around you*
- *Keep your eyes and ears open for what the other person really means. Remember to use active listening.*
- *If someone else has a habit you don't like (and maybe you have it too?), keep calm and ask yourself how it might, in some cases, be useful or attractive.*

WHAT DO I NEED?

Genuine interest in another person and the world around; a desire to look into yourself and to establish good relations with others.

HOW LONG WILL IT TAKE?

Special time is not necessary. Use these skills always in communication.

WHAT'S THE BENEFIT?

You will learn to see each person not as a representative but as an individual, different from others; and can learn to see positive traits in yourself and others. It will enrich your world and expand the circle of friends.

Suggest to friends during the week to work on identifying and overcoming stereotypes in their dealings with people. It will be interesting if they record some of their observations.

Education has a unique opportunity to influence the stereotypes of young people, and consequently, the future of those nations to which these young people belong. Sustainable development requires education to be diverse, reflecting the cultural and ethnic diversity of humankind, satisfying the comprehensive needs of different social and professional groups, as well as individual spiritual needs.

Students can learn skills of intercultural communication, communicative and empathic skills that allow such interaction, the understanding of "otherness", to foster openness to the perception of foreign cultures and ideological models. It is possible to ask students questions like: Do we always respect the opinions and views of others, their feelings, rights and needs? How, in what way shall we respect them? Is it important that another person accepts your views? Or shall I accept her/his point of view?

Opening up for awareness of our stereotypes is a critical function of learning for sustainability, at any age.

HEALTH AND WELLBEING

According to the World Health Organization, health is characterized not only by an absence of disease, but also a feeling of complete physical, mental and social wellbeing. Health is intimately connected with wellbeing, in the shape of a productive, creative, happy life. Wellbeing and health are each other's prerequisites and results, i.e. in the best case they are linked in a benevolent circle.

While ill-health (physical or otherwise) is regarded as a matter for treatment, and thus for specialists and infrastructure, good health remains the prerogative of the individual. Yet often, modern people take little or no action to preserve their own health; on the contrary, many indulge in health-destroying habits.

That is why many school curricula for education for sustainable development include health issues, including prevention of harmful habits. Students are invited to perform very simple actions regarding their daily habits and inclinations; for example, to use local products, try healthier food, refrain from addictive substances, enjoy physical exercise.

It is also important to introduce students of all ages to different aspects of a healthy lifestyle, empowering them to take an active role in securing their own health. 'Empowering' is indeed a key word in this context. A person who feels powerless to influence his or her daily life may find it difficult to adopt a healthy lifestyle, and may be an easy prey for addictive behaviour.

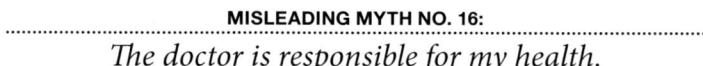

MISLEADING MYTH NO. 16:

The doctor is responsible for my health.

Economic sustainability

Economic sustainability is the most difficult of the three pillars to understand, because the entire economic system on which our societies are built is both unsustainable and irrational. Simply, it is hard to imagine that we have allowed our lives to be dominated by such insubstantial thought-forms.

Few disciplines are as shrouded in mist and myths as economics. At the very foundation of economics, the idea – often taken for granted – that there are immutable economic 'laws' is a dangerous myth.

A myth, because after all, people invented money. WE invented money, and it obeys only the 'laws' we invent for it; or, rather, it follows the rules we jointly agree upon.

Dangerous, because it leads us to accept unquestioningly the extraordinary idea that we cannot 'afford' to remedy what is obviously wrong, like extreme poverty, environmental destruction, and inadequate health and education services; while we somehow, mysteriously, can 'afford' a life of unparalleled luxury for a minority.

We can and must de-mythify money, and re-invent it, now that it no longer serves us in its present form.

Money obeys immutable laws analogous to the laws of nature.

THE UNDERLYING MYTH: ECONOMIC 'LAWS'

Economic 'laws' are often put forward as reasons for unsustainable behaviour. How is it that these laws seem to dictate that the rich can afford endless supplies of luxury (i.e. unnecessary for human welfare) goods, while the poor cannot 'afford' even the means to survive with dignity? How is it that the rich world can afford to fuel an endless spiral of increasing resource use, but not to pay the full cost of the resulting environmental degradation – nor indeed to fully fund essential services for its own citizens, like schools and health care?

In fact, where does money come from? And who decides where it goes? Even the true answers to these fundamental questions are contrary to what most people believe. The answers are as simple as they are surprising.

CREATING MONEY

Anyone who has a credit card understands that no gold is today involved in 'creating' money. Money-creating power has passed from the national banks to the banking system, i.e. private companies. Each time you or I borrow money, we enable the lending institution to 'create' that money. It's sometimes referred to as "debt money", because interest is charged by the lender to the borrower.

The next question is: who or what guarantees that money? It suited governments to drop the gold standard, but then how could they convince people it was safe to trade in their currencies? Answer: by creating a 'bank guarantee' funded by taxes that rescues any bank on the verge of bankruptcy. So in fact, you and I guarantee the money. When banks do well, they keep the profits. When they lose, we pay. (ref Lietaer)

This system is clearly not the result of any immutable economic 'laws', but of political (i.e. human) decisions. Some of the fruits of the system were harvested in

2008-11, when banks in many countries failed and huge government subsidies only served to conserve the same, unsustainable system. Such huge amounts of money, spent more wisely, could have put the whole of humanity on a more sustainable path. Is it really so hard to imagine a different system?

WHERE MONEY GOES

It takes only simple mathematics to work out that a "debt money" system inevitably results in the rich becoming, on average, richer.

The founding fathers of both Christianity and Islam forbade the charging of excessive interest, which has been variously interpreted as being anything above about 4 % – sometimes claimed to be a reasonable approximation of the natural yield of agriculture and forestry. Today's levels are much higher, even if you get what appears to be a cheap bank loan.

If, for instance, you buy a newly-built house in western Europe or the United States, probably about 40 % of the price you pay represents interest. Not only the interest you pay to the banks, but also the interest paid by the builder, and everyone else in the production chain. (ref Kennedy)

ONE LAW: THE INEVITABILITY OF ECONOMIC CRASHES

Other so-called economic laws may be mythical, but it is easy to understand that a debt-fuelled economy is bound to crash, periodically:

"Those who recognize the impossibility of perpetual exponential growth and who understand how compound interest is built into the global system of money and banking, expect the continuation of periodic "bubbles" and "busts," each of increasing amplitude until the system shakes itself apart.

66 *"Engineers call this phenomenon "positive feedback." Such a system cannot find equilibrium. Imagine a heating system in which the thermostat, sensing a rise in temperature, calls for more heat instead of less. Such is the nature of the debt-money system. The imposition of interest on the debt by which money is created, demands that more debt be created. Such is the debt imperative which gives rise to a growth imperative. Among other things, it prevents the emergence of a steady state economy."* — THOMAS H. GRECO, JR. (REF)

A debt-fuelled money system is not a 'law of nature' (or even of economics). But when allowed to flourish unchallenged, it does inevitably lead to greater and greater differences between rich and poor. This is in itself an important component of UNsustainable development.

IF THOSE ARE THE PROBLEMS, WHAT ARE THE SOLUTIONS?

This section has so far focused on economic (un)sustainability, without looking at the new, growing discipline of 'ecological economics'. If this expression sounds odd, it may be because the two words actually mean the same thing - or at least are derived from the same root: care for our home (oikos).

In fact several new disciplines have emerged in our universities and workplaces. From Wikipedia:

Ecological economics is a transdisciplinary field of academic research that aims to address the interdependence and coevolution of human economies and natural ecosystems over time and space. It is distinguished from environmental economics, which is the mainstream economic analysis of the environment, by its treatment of the economy as a subsystem of the ecosystem and its emphasis upon preserving natural capital. One survey of German economists found that ecological and environmental economics are different schools of economic thought, with ecological economists emphasizing "strong" sustainability and rejecting the proposition that natural capital can be substituted by human-made capital. The related field of green economicsis, in general, a more politically applied form of ecological economics.

For the purposes of this book we will look more closely only at those solutions that can be useful and accessible for groups of ordinary citizens.

INTENTIONAL ECONOMICS

Eric Beinhocker, an advisor to McKinsey, is another economics expert who points out that neoclassical economics is fundamentally flawed and has a poor record of empirical validation. Beinhocker claims (ref) that neoclassical theory is in the process of being supplanted by what he calls 'complexity economics' - the view that the economy is 'a complex adaptive system made up of realistically rational agents who dynamically interact with each other in an evolutionary system'.

'There's a systemic bias in money flow,' agrees Bernard Lietaer, Belgian professor of macro economics. (ref) 'It's against sustainable development. There's a whole new scientific field waiting to be created – the field of intentional economics.'

'Intentional economics' stands for a theory and practice of economics that puts money at the service of the long-term wellbeing of humanity: a monetary system that would enable us not to predict what money will do, but to use it to design the society we want.

Clearly a total economic collapse would be extremely painful - indeed, fatal for very many people. And this is probably the explanation for the continued support for neoclassical economics - this least sustainable of all human inventions. Any solutions need to work within the framework of the existing economic institutions, and either make them obsolete or transform them.

Many such solutions already exist. (ref Tsikota 2011) For instance LETS systems, which can be implemented by any group of people, small or large (old or young); and local, anti-inflationary bonds that can be implemented by any local authority (if permitted to do so). Mutual loan funds had such a function at one time, as did mutual insurance funds - see 'Peer to peer credit'.

LETS SYSTEMS

A 'local employment and trading system' is based on the observation that in any society, and particularly in one with economic difficulties such as unemployment, there are many people with skills and time to offer, and many people with unfilled needs - but no conventional money to link the two.

A LETS system brings the two together via a ledger or a computer system that allows each 'seller' to advertise their goods or services, and each person to act as both a buyer and a seller. Over time, the plus and minus for each person is expected to zero out: you sell as much as you buy via the system.

Most LETS systems to date are very local, and though some have existed for 20 years or more they are so far not significant in transforming economic systems. They do however often transform the lives of their members; and they have the advantage of being easy to start and run, as long as a person or group is willing to take responsibility for the exchange system.

There are also growing numbers of such systems operating between businesses, particularly small ones; there is even an international association for such systems. Indeed, it has been argued that the full potential of LETS systems will not be realized until there are national and international 'clearing houses' to enable wider trading.

LOCAL CURRENCIES

One step beyond LETS systems is the officially-supported creation of a dual currency system, with a local currency as well as the national one. In some countries this is illegal, despite its obvious advantages, and many initiatives in this direction have been effectively closed down by national bank authorities.

It is worth noting in this context that 'national banks' are not normally publicly-owned but are privately-owned, for-profit institutions that have usually been given a monopoly on currency creation, for reasons not connected with any idea of the social efficacy of the system.

Brazil is probably the first government to take strong action to support local currencies: the Banco do Brazil (Brazil's central bank) is multiplying this model at the rate of 10 a month, and planned to complete introduction in many more locations in the country.

Originally an initiative of local citizens in an impoverished northern district, with NGO support and now with government backing, the Brazilian dual currency system is creating thousands of jobs and lifting tens of thousands of people out of extreme poverty.

PEER-TO-PEER CREDIT

Once, 'mutual funds' had an important role in many societies. When you had a little surplus money, you saved it; when you needed money, you borrowed - to the extent that your and other people's savings made it possible. If a bank or other company was involved, it was to provide a service to you and your peers.

Such funds evolved from village or clan-based systems for sharing surplus wealth, and in particular for handling unusual or unexpected expenses.

Chris Cook points out that a modern version of such a system would also de-couple 'credit' from money creation:

"We are used to thinking that money must necessarily 'be' credit. In fact, while credit (meaning, time to pay) is a necessary part of a monetary system, credit need not - indeed, should not, be 'monetised'... The approach I advocate is of mutually guaranteed 'Peer to Peer' credit within the framework of a mutual guarantee agreement."

In this system users would have guarantee limits, rather than credit limits, and may settle credit not just in conventional money but in money's worth of goods, services, or other obligations. No interest is charged, but both sellers and buyers pay a service charge and a provision into a default pool. The "Pool" is owned mutually, not by the bank - though today's banks might become providers of the services to keep the system running.

CARE FOR OUR HOME: NOTHING IS INEVITABLE

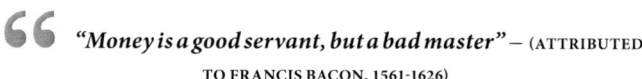 *"Money is a good servant, but a bad master"* – (ATTRIBUTED TO FRANCIS BACON, 1561-1626)

The point of this chapter on economic sustainability is twofold: to point out some of the major misunderstandings, or myths, about money and economics; and to make the point that nothing is inevitable (except, under the present system, bank crashes). There are alternatives, and many of them can be used by small groups of people without intervention from national or international agencies.

One of the most urgent challenges of sustainable development is to create better and better ways of handling economics. Education for sustainable development needs to equip students to think critically about existing systems, and explore new solutions.

Environmental sustainability

The whole concept of sustainable development is often, in people's minds, linked to 'environment'; the other aspects are often invisible.

Even within the area of ecological sustainability, one aspect is often emphasized at the expense of others. For instance, in 2009 the two most-publicized concepts were 'global warming' – more correctly called 'global climate change', which indeed has gained currency since then; and 'peak oil'.

GLOBAL CLIMATE CHANGE

The world has entered a period of climatic instability, linked to sharp increases in concentrations of carbon dioxide (CO_2) in the atmosphere. The general trends are for
- *Warmer weather, though changes are unevenly distributed across the globe*
- *Less predictable weather*
- *Increasing occurrences of extreme weather conditions, like typhoons*
- *Rising sea levels*

There is no longer any question about these trends. Indeed, an august expert geological commission has announced, in 2009, (ref Zalasiewicz et al) that 'The Holocene era is now at an end'.

A few scientists still maintain that the change is not (solely) due to human intervention, by the release of CO2 into the atmosphere, but is to a large extent the result of 'normal' fluctuations. Their scepticism is however of little relevance for sustainable development: a link has been proved between the climate change and CO2 concentrations in the atmosphere; the climate change is negative for almost all humans; humans are pushing CO2 into the atmosphere in historically unparalleled quantities. Shouldn't that be a sufficient basis on which to decide that it could be good to slow down CO2 emissions?

INCREASING VULNERABILITY

The focus on climate change per se tends to obscure the fact that we are at the same time making ourselves more and more vulnerable to the effects of the climate change.

- *More and more people crowd into cities, increasing the risks associated with almost any environmental hazard*
- *More and more people live very close to the sea, exposing themselves not only to such relatively rare phenomena as tsunamis, but also to rising sea levels and the many sea-engendered weather effects like tornados/typhoons and extreme tides*
- *More and more trees are cut down, exposing hillsides – and the people who live on or below them – to violent weather effects*
- *More and more rivers are 'tamed': straightened, dammed and otherwise changed in ways that reduce their capacity to absorb or buffer unusual water levels*

The list, which could be made much longer, demonstrates clearly that ecological sustainability cannot be separated from social and economic sustainability.

SAVING THE PLANET?

Another way of looking at ecological sustainability is to see it as a pressing need to 'save the planet'. But does the planet need saving? Not really.

It's not about saving trees, or whales, or the planet – or even 'life on earth'. Life on earth existed for billions of years before we humans came along, and will probably continue long after we leave. Or, to paraphrase a biologist: If all the insects on the planet were to die, all other life would also die. If all the humans on the planet were to die, almost no-one else would notice.

What this whole sustainability discussion is about, is whether or not we can secure a future for the human race; and preferably a future in which people will feel comfortable.

The list of problems above may look daunting. Indeed, some people are asking whether it is not already too late. Have we already passed humanity's 'best before' date? No-one can answer that question. But we can ask others, instead:
- *If I act, in my daily life, as if it's already too late, how does that affect the outcome?*
- *And if I act as if it's not too late, how does that affect the outcome?*

We can probably safely say that if many or most people choose the first option, the option to be a pessimist, then it almost certainly will be too late – soon, if not already. If many or most choose the optimist option, it may not be too late.

So there are good, practical reasons to choose to be an optimist. Besides, optimists have more fun.

MISLEADING MYTHS NOS. 19 & 20

Sustainable development is about saving the planet. It's already too late – human society is doomed.

MEASURING PROGRESS

How do we find out whether we are heading in the right direction? How can we measure sustainability - or unsustainability?

One answer is: by measuring our ecological footprints.

The idea behind the ecological footprint is that all human impact on our environment can be equated to land area - to square metres or hectares or football pitches. Each of us needs land to grow our food, to live on, to travel on, to take care of our garbage, and not least to absorb all the carbon dioxide and other bye-products of our lifestyles.

A country has an ecological footprint. In the case of the Netherlands, for instance, it is several times the size of the country: such a heavily populated country needs to import many things it needs, including 'air space': land and plants to absorb carbon dioxide and ensure a supply of breathable air.

A city or region also has an ecological footprint that can be calculated. And so does a household, and an individual - and a product. Average personal footprints are calculated annually for almost every country on the planet, and compared with available resources.

With the help of the ecological footprint we can understand that we are already in debt to nature. The plants on which we (and all other animals) depend are overworked. Before the end of each year, we collectively have used up more than all the plants on the planet are able to produce in a year (ref Roberts). For the rest of the year, we are drawing on reserves - like a prodigal heir, day by day using up the capital he has inherited, so that finally there will be nothing left for future generations.

So one way of describing the search for environmental sustainability is to say that we will reduce our ecological footprint, to a size that fits on the planet, and which gives us a margin: the space we need to restore natural capital.

PEAK EVERYTHING

'Peak oil' means that the extraction of fossil oil from below the earth or sea has passed (or soon will pass) its peak. Never again will it be possible to extract oil at the rates of… well, recent years.

Clearly this affects many things, not only availability but also price. Only a few years ago, the idea of oil ever costing as much as 100 USD a barrel was regarded as some kind of science fiction. In July 2008 the price passed 140 USD a barrel, and there are forecasts that it will pass 200 USD within a decade.

Mathis Wackernagel (ref) makes the point that the focus on peak oil obscures other important 'peak' conditions. He says it's more a question of 'peak everything':

"We are facing not only peak oil, but also peak water, peak food, and more – so, focussing on climate change/carbon alone may be a tactical mistake. 'Peak Everything' compels us to be more holistic in our thinking and evaluation, particularly to avoid perverse outcomes. Trying to solve seemingly discrete issues, or jumping to quick fixes without a whole-system and long term view, could create even more problems."

ECOLOGICAL IMPERATIVES

'You can't negotiate with a living cell,' says Karl-Henrik Robért, founder of The Natural Step. 'Either it will survive in a given environment, or it will not.' (ref)

The Natural Step has formulated three fundamental ecological 'system conditions', a development of the principles of ecology propounded a century ago by The British Ecological Society; and has added a fourth condition concerned with social sustainability (q.v.). In essence, they are
1. Stop extracting minerals from the earth's crust: they shall not be allowed to continue to accumulate in the biosphere

2. Stop manufacturing and releasing into the biosphere substances that do not occur in nature
3. Stop diminishing our natural capital
4. Ensure the opportunity for every person to have access to the necessities of life

These principles imply radical changes to current practice. The first principle, for example, if fully adopted would lead to the end of all mining and drilling extractions. How would we live without iron, and the many other metals on which our society depends? One answer is of course 'recycling': we need to learn how to 'mine' our own garbage, and make new use of existing resources.

Encouragingly, more and more businesses are beginning to implement these system conditions (see Different arenas, different examples). Human inventiveness is so great that once the necessity is acknowledged, no doubt solutions will be found.

This is not the same thing as saying that 'technology will solve all environmental problems,' and turning away from the problems. Very specifically, technology can solve technical problems such as those embodied in principles 1 and 2. And will do so, when and if we as a society give priority to these problems.

MISLEADING MYTH NO. 21:

If enough money is invested in research and development, technology will bring about a sustainable society.

BUT WHAT ABOUT NATURE?

Is 'nature education' not a part of sustainable development? Yes indeed.

In fact, it's the heart of the matter. When we lose our connection with nature, when we begin to believe that nature is something 'out there' and separate from us, then we are lost. Not only metaphorically but also literally. On the other hand, experience of a connection with nature is in itself restorative:

> ❝ *[R]esearch shows that nature can offer powerful therapy for such maladies as depression, obesity, and attention-deficit disorder. Environment-based education dramatically improves standardized test scores and grade-point averages and develops skills in problem solving, critical thinking, and decision making. Anecdotal evidence strongly suggests that childhood experiences in nature stimulate creativity.*❞ — RICHARD LOUV (REF)

Note that we are here talking about something different from a conventional lesson. Once again, as with other aspects of ESD, transfer of knowledge is not the primary objective.

Learning to connect with (the rest of) nature can be and is done in many ways. Just a few examples:
- *To experience the outdoors at different seasons, weather, times of day*
- *To experience different landscapes, and their inhabitants*
- *To become acquainted with plants and animals living in cities*
- *To visit farms and find out where most food starts its life*
- *To forage for food without damage*
- *To take responsibility for plants or animals in need of care*

This is not necessarily easy, or indeed uncontroversial. Much depends on the attitude and values of the educator. In a critique of Louv, Michael Vandeman (ref) writes:

> 66 *It should be obvious (but apparently isn't) that how we interact with nature determines how we think about it and how we learn to treat it. Remember, children don't learn so much what we tell them, but they learn very well what they see us do. Fishing, building "forts", mountain biking, and even berry-picking teach us that nature exists for us to exploit."*

'Wilderness' experiences, either alone or in groups, are in many cultures the basis for rituals and rites of passage, recognizing our need to connect with other species - to the extent that they will allow us, and with due respect for their as well as our need for security.

So, nature education starts with spending time outdoors and can have different focuses such as gaining intimate knowledge of a small space (forest, waterside, meadow, vacant city lot, park, 'green' school yard) over time; meeting and greeting other species; caring for plants and animals (also indoors); exploring relationships between species - including who eats what (or whom). However it's done, it's a question of recovering our sense of ourselves as an inextricable part of nature.

MISLEADING MYTH NO. 22:
··

Nature is something else, separate from humans.

Values and worldview

Vandeman, quoted in the previous section, criticizes a view of our natural environment that emphasizes its usefulness for us humans. It is certainly true that humans are currently over-exploiting the assets produced by other species - see for instance the concept of 'overshoot'. It may also be true that this over-exploitation is underpinned by our reluctance or inability to quantify just how useful, or indeed essential, those other species are.

This is one approach to reducing over-exploitation: to make it uneconomic by putting a realistic price on it. Increasingly, in the overlap between economic and environmental sustainability, we find such concepts as 'ecosystem services' (Hawken, 2010): the idea that nature supplies humankind with valuable (indeed, invaluable because life-supporting) services that are currently being eroded by humans. See also the section on Natural capital.

This concept was systematized in the United Nations Millennium Ecosystem Assessment, a four-year study involving more than 1,300 scientists worldwide. It grouped ecosystem services into four broad categories:
- *Provisioning, such as the production of food and water*
- *Regulating, such as the control of climate and disease*
- *Supporting, such as nutrient cycles and crop pollination*
- *Cultural, such as spiritual and recreational benefits*

At the societal level there is much discussion and some action about 'costing' - assigning a value to ecosystem services - and payment. That is, humans (individuals, businesses, government) making use of and/or degrading such services should pay for them (ref Dept. for Environment Food and Rural Affairs). In the case of severe degradation, the cost could be so high that no-one would be able to afford it.

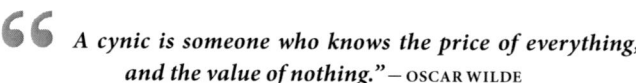

> *A cynic is someone who knows the price of everything,*
> *and the value of nothing."* — OSCAR WILDE

At the educational level there are interesting questions to be pursued, such as
- *How much is it worth to have access to clean air, water, soil?*
- *How clean is clean enough? How do we know?*
- *Is there anything that can be done to improve the current situation?*

An interesting topic here is that of 'the commons': naturally available benefits that are assumed to be common property - until such time as a person or group 'fences them in'. A large body of literature is growing around the idea that it should be possible to reverse the current trend, which is to fence in more and more of the commons: not only to safeguard essential ecosystem services but also to make more and more intellectual property freely available. Computer programs can be free; books, reports, music, film can be made freely available for downloading; technical innovations can be made freely available. These counter-trends are often referred to as 'open source' or 'open access'.

There is a strong connection between 'open access' and a revitalization of democracy - which brings us back to social sustainability.

Furthermore, such questions lead inevitably to the topic of ethics. There is a growing secular discussion on 'climate ethics' (ref Gardiner et al) and other ethical dimensions of (un)sustainable development. The basic principles involved – respect for natural, human and social capital – are also expressed in more technical, utilitarian terms as for instance in Contraction and Convergence.

Many spiritual and religious movements are also, or are becoming, champions of sustainable development. In this they echo an increasing public frustration, in many parts of the world, with what is perceived as political impotence and commercial greed. The qualities they frequently advocate and promote, in common with secular social sustainability movements, are stewardship of natural resources, and solidarity – in other words, care for natural and social capital.

HAPPINESS INDEX

The question of what we value is closely linked to the question of prosperity, which in turn leads to the question of what makes us happy - or unhappy. For instance, does money make us happy? Clearly not (ref Diener); yet the only globally-accepted measure of prosperity is money, or gross domestic product (GDP).

> 66 *[G]ross domestic product should no longer be the only serious index of how well a nation is doing. It is not just the alarming divergence between quality of life and GDP that warrants this conclusion. Policy itself follows from what is measured, and if all that is measured is money, all policy will be about getting more money."* — MARTIN SELIGMAN

> 66 *We are stealing the future, selling it in the present, and calling it GDP."* — PAUL HAWKEN

In 1972, HM King Jigme Singye Wangchuk of Bhutan suggested introducing a 'gross national happiness' index, or GNH. A measuring system was developed based on the following factors:

- *Physical, mental and spiritual health*
- *Time-balance*
- *Social and community vitality*
- *Cultural vitality*
- *Education*
- *Living standards*
- *Good governance*
- *Ecological vitality*

The index is used in Bhutan as the basis for all national planning. For instance, proposed policies must pass a GNH review based on a GNH impact statement.

A simpler measurement, called the Happy Planet Index, has been developed by The New Economics Foundation, which annually publishes ranking lists covering most countries in the world. It builds on three factors:

- *Health, expressed in life expectancy*
- *Ecological footprint*
- *Subjective assessments of wellbeing by inhabitants*

In an educational context, this topic can supply many interesting discussion points. For instance,

- *Think of an occasion when you started the day feeling happy and optimistic - what made you feel that way? What were you feeling?*
- *When you started the day feeling 'heavy' and unwilling - what made you feel that way?*

How do you feel when setting off for work or school? How do you feel when you read a newspaper or watch the TV news? When do you feel most/least energetic?

We have found that for most people there is a very clear social dimension to wellbeing. Friendship, mutual support, small acts of consideration and kindness, the many daily aspects of interaction with other people are all important components of wellbeing.

AS ON THE INSIDE, SO ON THE OUTSIDE

Another way of looking at sustainability is to see the present problematical situation as a direct reflection of our collective inner chaos and disconnection from real things happening in the real world.

It's not quite as simple as saying that if we all slow down and learn to meditate, everything will solve itself. But it does seem reasonable to suppose that if many more people become aware - of themselves and of everything around them - then the demand for many, many environmentally disruptive products and services will drop in proportion.

After all, would you really choose to buy a banana if you knew someone had died producing it? Or a piece of furniture made from illegally-logged rainforest wood, if you knew the consequences? Would you need to buy a new motorbike of the latest model, despite having one that functions well? Would you buy a cheap shirt if you knew that child slaves had been forced to make it?

> **❝ ❞** *Why should I spend money I don't have, on things I don't need, to impress people I don't care about?"* — T J STRINKO

These seemingly unrelated questions can point the way to a golden pedagogical opportunity. The important thing is not that the students take one particular action rather than another, but that they learn

- *To see themselves, individually and in groups, as a sustainability factor to be reckoned with*
- *To allow themselves to find out about and reflect upon cause and effect, even when the results are uncomfortable*
- *To embark on an inner dialogue about what is really important to them*

TRIPLE-LOOP LEARNING: THE JOURNEY CONTINUES

Marilyn:

Is the world getting better, or worse? A case can certainly be made for either position. Importantly, at this time, it does seem that the ground breaking, mind-shifting work of creating a new, sustainable society is slower than the pace at which unsustainable practices are spreading.

> 66 *The outer boundary of what we currently believe is feasible is still far short of what we actually must do."*
> — AL GORE, NOBEL ACCEPTANCE, DECEMBER 10, 2007

About 15 years into our grand experiment with ESD, which started in 1990, we began to ask ourselves why - despite our acclaimed successes - progress was so slow. Only a million or two people enrolled in our programs? So little apparent interest in learning better ways to run programs for sustainable development?

In fact, by the end of the 20th century the world was full of databases of 'good' or even 'best' SD practice, and to no apparent effect. Almost every SD project around the world started from Base Zero, reinventing the wheel and sometimes even proving to their own satisfaction the impossibility of the task. In other words, globally, projects and programs for sustainable development are so far not very effective because they make very poor use of the experience and resources available to them.

We started looking for common factors; both success and failure factors. We continued analysing and synthesizing - and looking for better ways to do it. A small R&D group met regularly and explored tools and methods.

The two most powerful tools we found were 'pattern language', originally developed to help architects and urban planners to avoid reinventing too many wheels; and community-based research as a model for how small groups can be empowered to transform their own reality. The third tool was one we were already using and developing ourselves, namely 'empowerment'.

From these three came the concept of a specific kind of meeting or workshop with the purpose of enabling project participants to understand and explain their own experience in terms of driving and hindering forces. And not only to reach these conclusions, but to do it quickly and effectively, and to document them in a way that makes the experience accessible to others.

Now we have tested this approach, currently called Learning for Change, in a variety of countries and situations. Even though still under development, it is yielding some impressive results.

Experiences with 'Learning for Change'

The Learning for Change methodology is an attempt to create a systematic approach to triple-loop learning: not only examining and appraising what we have learnt (double-loop learning) but also describing it in ways that make it accessible to others. (ref Argyris) It is time to learn not only from our own experience but also from that of others.

> 66 *"In a constantly changing environment, sustainability is not some ultimate endpoint but ... a continuous process of learning and adaptation. Designing for sustainability not only requires the re-design of our habits, lifestyles and practices, but also, the way we think about design. ... The transition towards sustainability is about co-creating a human civilization that flourishes within the ecological limits of the planetary life support system."* — DANIEL WAHL

CO-CREATION IS A WHOLE WORLD AWAY FROM 'IMPROVEMENTS'

The enormous challenge of this work is that we need to find ways to leap-frog. It's not enough to learn to do the same things better – we need to learn in ways that help us leap to new insights, new solutions and new effectiveness. Every time. A basic condition is the need to raise our awareness.

'Awareness' can be interpreted at many levels of human being. At every level, it can help us towards sustainable development. In the workshops we turn our attention to a specific kind of awareness: awareness of our patterns of behaviour and in particular the mental patterns that dictate our behaviour – in the absence of awareness.

One of the entry points is to identify recurring problems. A frequently occurring problem hints at underlying patterns. For instance, 'We've informed everyone at least five times about the importance of sorting their garbage, but still they don't do it!' This can be related to a generic problem well known to educators, 'They don't do as I say!' One equally well-known response to this is that in general pupils do what you do, not what you say – which indeed is a part of the pattern, though not the whole. This pattern has many facets, and seeing them described in a systematic way can help in finding or generating appropriate solutions.

A STRUCTURED PROCESS

Originally intended as a tool for improved projects for SD, the Learning for Change methodology has evolved into two modes, and is also being adapted for use specifically in an educational setting. In all cases it involves a structured process, designed to identify problems or concerns, and then

- *Ask questions in order to uncover underlying patterns; for instance 'Why is this a problem?', or 'Is this something we recognize from other situations?'*
- *Formulate 'a better way': how to avoid or resolve the problems in the future.*

The process alternates between analysis and synthesis, which means that it makes unusual demands on participants. We are accustomed, in educational systems, to teaching and learning analysis, but synthesis is rarely introduced.

This in itself reflects a significant dysfunctional pattern of western civilization, namely the belief that a problem can (always) best be understood by breaking it down into discrete parts. This belief underpins the industrial revolution, among many other phenomena, and is integral to most of our education systems; it is however a distinct hindrance when attempting to understand and teach for sustainable development.

TWO KINDS OF WORKSHOP

A 'Learning for Change' process can bring together people from different projects and countries, each with their own case from which to learn: or it can bring together stakeholders in a single project or program.

Marilyn:

A milestone for the single-project approach was when the Swedish team travelled to Kiev in 2007 to work with Olena and her teachers' team to evaluate the first phase of the Lessons for SD project.

One thing we learnt was in fact NOT to refer to the workshop as an evaluation meeting. A typical evaluation meeting is characterized by a certain defensiveness and a desire to show everything in the best possible light, often at the expense of reality. A 'Learning for Change' workshop, on the other hand, is explicitly designed to distill knowledge from the participants, and we found at the Kiev event that they had indeed accumulated a huge amount of knowledge during the project - and were enabled to formulate it in a period so short that it surprised all of us. Less than two days were required.

The first major multinational, multi-case workshop was held together with SWEDESD (ref) in Sweden in 2009 (video). Since then the number of events has multiplied, with participants mainly from Europe, Asia and Africa, and the method has been successively refined. A facilitator training component has been added.

> ❝ *The sessions were eye opening and it was a rich experience of working with teacher trainers from a wide region. My greatest moment was to see the passion of learning as expressed by both the facilitators and the learners. It confirmed the social aspect of learning. I got some new ideas /that/ will be very valuable in the presentations I make. I sit in the Academic Committee at the institution and I want to model some of the aspects such as the Synergy meeting so that I can empower the educational leaders to implement the approach in their departments.*

> ❝ *I have talked to my colleague from Uganda and I am thinking of collaborating with him on his water project. I am also considering working with a colleague from Swaziland whose institutional project on water could be exchanged with mine on electricity and see how we can address both utilities at our institutions.*" — GIOKO ANTHONY, VICE PRINCIPAL: PD AND OUTREACH, AGA KHAN ACADEMY, MOMBASA

Olena:

Many but not all of the participants at our workshops have been educators: teachers, teacher trainers, youth leaders, and so on. They are beginning to report on how they are adapting the method to classroom work, both with pupils and for teacher training.

This method will be the subject of separate publications. Reports are also available or under development from multi-case-study, multinational workshops in Sweden, Vietnam, South Africa, Norway, India.

CASE: SCHOOLS IN UGANDA USE LEARNING FOR CHANGE

Ronald Ddungu is deputy principal of a school for girls in Uganda. He began to introduce L4C with a voluntary weekend workshop for especially interested pupils. Their enthusiasm was infectious – 'ALL pupils should be taught to work like this!' – and has led to first teachers and then the entire pupil body embarking on a journey to discover more effective ways to learn.

The experience is now spreading within the school district: in May 2012, writes Ronald Ddungu, "I had a workshop for Principals and two of their teachers from selected schools, totalling 130 participants". (photos)

Sustainability begins at home

The journey begins with ourselves. 'Be the change you want to see,' said Gandhi. Or, as a Sufi sage put it several centuries ago:

> 66 *"Everything begins with remembering. Caught between the immensity of the universe, and the trivia of everyday living, we forget who we truly are."* — SHEIKH ISMAIL HAKKI

A sustainable lifestyle is not something you preach, or even teach. It is to be lived, from moment to moment, not as a perfected state but as an adventure into the unknown.

This is perhaps easier said than done. So many of us have lost our childhood senses of wonder, curiosity, and discovery; sacrificed them at the altar of 'knowledge'. It can be very difficult to acknowledge that what we 'know', in any absolute sense, is very small in relation to what remains to be discovered.

It can be even more difficult to accept that the chaotic situation we humans have created on our planet is a reflection of the chaos inside us: a reflection of our fears, aggressions, greed, isolation. If we take another look at the world around us we can also see other reflections: of our love, hope, empathy, generosity, connectedness. The inner work of sustainable development is about "remembering who we truly are" - loving, generous spirits - and learning to radiate more of that awareness into the world around us.

REFERENCES

Argyris, Chris et al. Triple-Loop Learning. Authentic Learning International, 2010.

Assagioli, R. The Act of Will. New York: England Penguin Books, 1973.

AtKisson, Alan. "Amoeba: a model for culture change." 2001.

Beinhocker, Eric. Origin of Wealth : Evolution, Complexity, and the Radical Remaking of Economics. Boston, USA: Harvard Business School Press, 2007. Hardback.

Bergson, Henri. Athlone Contemporary European Thinkers Series. Continuum, 2002.

Brunner, Wolgang. "The Mission." Brunner, Wolfgang. Solvagnen: Verktyg Till Din Miljoundervisning. Stockholm: Liber Utbildning AB, 1997. 11-28.

Bussey, Marcus. "Global Education from a Neohumanist Perspective: A Musical Exposition." Journal of Futures Studies (August 2007): 12 (1) : 25-40.

Chomsky, Noam. Occupy. Zuccotti Park Press, 2012.

Crompton, Tom. "Weathercocks and Signposts", WWF 2008

Dept. for Environment Food and Rural Affairs. Payments for Ecosystem and Services, 2013

Dewey, John. How We Think. New York, USA: Dover Publications Inc., 1998. Paperback.

Diener, Ed. Happiness: Unlocking the Mysteries of Psychological Wealth. Wiley-Blackwell, 2008.

Downey, Myles. Effective coaching: lessons from the coach's coach. Florence, KY: Texere Publishing, 2003. Paperback.

Engdahl, Ingrid and Milada Rabušicová. Education for Sustainable Development in Practice. 2011.

Ferreira, Francisco Whitaker. Towards a New Politics: What Future for the World Social Forum? Zed Books, 2006.

Ferrucci, Piero. What We May Be: Techniques for psychological and spiritual growth through psychosysnthesis. Tarcher, 2009. Papereback.

Gardiner, Stephen et al. (ed) Climate Ethics, Oxford University Press, 2010

Gardner, Howard. Multiple Intelligences: New Horizons, The Development and Education of the Mind. Basic Books, 2006.

van Gelder, Sarah. "This changes everything", YES! Magazine, 2012

Gershon, David and Gail Straub. Empowerment: The Art of Creating Your Life as You Want it. Stering Ethos, 2011.

Goleman, Daniel. Emotional Intelligence. New York, NY: Bantam Books, 2006.

—. Vital lies, Simple truths: The psychology of self-deception. New York: Simon & Schuster, 1985.

Gordon, Thomas. Leader Effectiveness Training. New York: Wyden Books, 1977.

Greco, H Thomas, Jr. The End of Money and the Future of Civilisation. USA: Chelsea Green Publishing Company, 2009. Trade paper.

Halpern, D F. "Teaching for Critical Thinking: Helping College Students Develop the Skills and Dispositions of a Critical Thinker." New Directions for Teaching and Learning (1999): 69-74.

Hargreaves, Tom. "Changing Environmental Behaviour: a review of evidence from Global Action Plan", University of East Anglia, 2008

Harland, P and H J Staats. Effects of the EcoTeam Programme in the long term: the situation two years after participation. Leiden: Working group Energy and Environment, Rijksuniversiteit, 1997.

Harland, P, et al. "Explaining Proenvironmental Intention and Behavior by Personal Norms and the Theory of Planned Behavior." Journal of Applied Social Psychology (1999): 2505-2528.

Hart, Elizabeth and Meg Bond. Action research for health and social care: A guide to practice. (Buckingham and Philadelphia): Open University Press, 1995.

Hawken, P, B Lovins Amory and Hunter Lovins L. Natural Capitalism: The Next Industrial Revolution. London: Earthscan, 2010. Paperback.

Hawken, Paul. "Reimagining the World Was a Responsibility". Greenbiz.com, 2011.

Heath, C and Heath D. Switch: How to Change Things When Change is Hard. New York, NY: Broadway Books, 2010. Paperback.

Inayatullah, Sohail. Questioning the Future: Futures studies, Action Learning and Organizational Transformation. Tamsui: Tamang University, 2002.

Jacometti, S A. Creating and Sustaining a Behaviour Change in Energy Conservation. Masters thesis. London, UK: Imperial College, 2009.

Jorsäter, Esbjörn, Marilyn Mehlmann, Lydia Pshenitsyna, Irina Semko, Ivan Tsikota. Drawing for Life, 2012.

Kaushik, Helena. "People: From Impoverishment to Empowerment." American Journal of Economics and Sociology (1996): 160-162.

Kennedy, Margrit. Interest and Inflation Free Money: An Exchange Medium That Works for Everybody. Philadelphia, PA, USA: New Society Publishers, 1995. Paperback.

Korten, David C. Agenda for a New Economy. Berrett-Koelher, 2nd edition, 2010.

—. The Great Turning. Berrett-Koehler, 2005.

Lappe, Frances Moore. EcoMind: Changing the Way We Think, to Create the World We Want. Nation Books, 2011.

Lietaer, Bernard and Jacqui Dunne. Rethinking Money: How New Currencies Turn Scarcity into Prosperity. Berrett-Koehler Publisher, Inc, 2013.

Lietaer, Bernard and M Kennedy. Monnaies régionales: De nouvelles voies vers une prospérité durable. Charles Leopold Mayer, 2008. Paperback.

Lietaer, Bernard. The Future Of Money: Towards Wealth, Work and Wiser World. Random House, 2002. Paperback.

Louv, R. Last Child in the Woods: Saving Our Children from Nature-Deficit Disorder. New York, USA: Algonquin Books of Chapel Hill, 2008. Paperback.

McLaren, Nadia, Marilyn Mehlmann and Olena Pometum. "Learning to Live Sustainably." Global Environmental Research Vol.14 No.2, 2010.

Meadows, Donella H, Jorgen Randers and Dennis L Meadows. Beyond the Limits: Confronting Global Collapse, Envisioning a Sustainable Future. Chelsea Green Publishing Company, 1993.

Mehlmann, Marilyn. "The Blind Men and the ESD Elephant." Ananda Marga Gurukula News, Issue 23, October 2006.

Mehlmann, Marilyn and Andre Benaim. Learning for Change. 2012.

Nadeau, Robert. "The Economist Has No Clothes: Unscientific assumptions in economic theory are undermining efforts to solve environmental problems." The Scientific American, March 2008

Neumayer, Eric. Weak versus Strong Sustainability: Exploring the Limits of two Opposing Paradigms. UK: Edward Elgar Publishing Limited, 2013.

Quilligan, James. "People Sharing Resources/ Toward a New Multilateralism of the Global Commons." Kosmos Journal, Fall/Winter 2009.

Rensselaer Polytechnic Institute: "Scientists Discover Tipping Point for the Spread of Ideas", Science Daily, July 26, 2011

Rheingold, Howard. Cultural Evolution of Human Cooperation: Summaries and Findings. Cambridge, MA: MIT Press, 2012.

Robért, Karl-Henrik. The Natural Step Story: Seeding a Quiet Revolution. New Catalyst Books, 2008.

Roberts, Carter. The day the earth ran out. Foreign Affairs, UK, 2013

Rogers, Everett M. Diffusion of Innovations. New York: Simon and Schuster, 2010. 4th Edition.

Rosenberg, Marshall. Nonviolent Communication: A language of Life. Puddledancer Press, 2003. 2th Edition.

Toomes, Anne Helen. A Transition to Sustainable Development: Empowerment and Disempowerment in a Nicaraguan Community. 2008.

Tsikota, Ivan. Increasing Local Economic Sustainability. Masters thesis, Stockholm University, 2011

Vandeman, Michael. Thoughts on the Book "Last Child in the Woods". The Thinking Mother, 2008

Wackernagel, Mathis, Living Well on One Planet, University of South Australia, 2008

Wackernagel, Mathis, Biocapacity, Footprint Network News, 2006

White, Alasdair. From Comfort Zone to Performance Management. Belgium: White & MacLean Publishing, 2009.

White, Clayton et al. Pattern Laboratory: pedagogy for sustainable development, 2009.

Zalasiewicz, Jan et al. GSA Today, 18 (2), 2008

Ziegler, Warren. Ways of Enspiriting: Transformative Practices for the Twenty-First Century. Spiritual Learning, 1995.

ACKNOWLEDGEMENTS

We are deeply indebted to our 'case study' owners,
to our colleagues

Andre Benaim
Marcus Bussey
Lotten Carlsson
Frans Lenglet
Nadia McLaren
Miriam Sannum
Igor Sushchenko
Ivan Tsikota
Clayton White

…and to many more from whom we are still learning.